GETTING ALONG WHEN YOU FEEL LIKE GETTING EVEN

GETTING *Along*
WHEN YOU FEEL LIKE
GETTING EVEN

What YOU Can Do to Resolve Conflict at Home, with Neighbors, in the Church, at Work, & with Difficult People

BERNARD K. BANGLEY

Harold Shaw Publishers
Wheaton, Illinois

ISBN 0-87788-367-X

Cover design by David LaPlaca

Library of Congress Cataloging-in-Publication Data

Bangley, Bernard. 1935-
    Getting along when you feel like getting even : what you can do to resolve conflict / Bernard Bangley.
      p. cm.
    ISBN 0-87788-367-X
    1. Conflict management—Religious aspects—Christianity.
    2. Interpersonal relations—Religious aspects—Christianity.
    3. Christian life—1960- I. Title.
    BV4597.53.C58B36 1993
    248.4—dc20   92-44253
                                            CIP

99 98 97 96 95 94 93

10 9 8 7 6 5 4 3 2 1

CONTENTS

1

WHY PEOPLE FIGHT

Pale Ebenezer thought it wrong to fight,
But Roaring Bill (who killed him) thought it right.
Hilaire Belloc, *The Pacifist*

The old bull moose snorted and lowered his head. His massive antlers made an impressive display. They were much broader and heavier than those of his young rival. From this new angle they looked like the side of a barn, or the front of a locomotive. The younger moose did not flinch. His heart may have been racing, but he stood his ground.

About thirty yards away a cow moose pretended to ignore the contest. She stood knee deep in water and calmly nibbled away at aquatic plants. But even a casual observer would understand that it was her presence and availability that prompted the bulls to square off against each other.

After a few grunts, puffs, and hoof scrapings, the big bull made a tentative lunge toward the younger one. It was dodged and returned. The animals were so massive that even small thrusts carried great power. After a minute or two of this kind of heavyweight sparring, the young bull saw an opening and took it. The injury was not severe enough to be fatal, but it drew blood. After a moment more of aggressive posturing, the older moose conceded defeat and sauntered off into the brush.

The young male did not chase him; he headed for the pond to claim his trophy.

I turned away from the TV. "That's the same thing you can see in any schoolyard," I commented to my wife.

She smiled, and I suddenly remembered our first date. I was eighteen, and she was a startlingly attractive seventeen. I took her to a movie theater in downtown Norfolk, Virginia. As we walked down the sidewalk to the box office, some sailors were leaning against parked cars. They began to whistle and make catcalls and breathy sounds of appreciation.

While that was probably not a new experience for her, it was a wild and threatening one for me. What was I supposed to do? Would I be required to defend her honor? Did she expect me to beat up half a dozen sailors on the pavement of their own port city? In my first hour with the girl I was going to marry it became clear to me that I would have competitors.

Even as I paid for our tickets, the muttering continued. My fear and uncertainty grew. I decided to follow Anna's lead. She ignored them; I ignored them, too. Soon enough we were safe inside. When the movie was over, I was relieved to see that the sailors were gone.

Why do we, as human beings, like to fight and compete? There are five main reasons—reasons we need to understand in order to get along most effectively with the difficult people in our lives.

We Fight Because We Are Biological Creatures

Sex is one of the primary triggers of serious combat. It starts a lot of fights. The precise details of what happened to the mutineers of the H.M.S. *Bounty* are clouded by myth and fiction. These facts, at least, are known: The British navy chased nine English sailors, six Tahitian men, and eleven Tahitian women to Pitcairn Island. They lived there in peace, far removed from the constraints of civilized society, for two years. Then two of the men got into a dispute over one of the women. After ten years on Pitcairn Island twelve of the fifteen men had been murdered. Peace returned to the island paradise when the population was reduced to one man, nine women, and twenty-five children.

In the natural world there is a struggle for reproductive success. The assumed purpose of this competitiveness, often leading to combativeness, is fitness. Stronger, more attractive individuals pass along the healthiest genes. The unsuccessful competitor has few or no offspring. Scientists call this "sexual selection."

Irrational Behavior
It is nothing less than snobbery to think that humans are somehow immune to the pressures forced upon us by our biological juices and genetic programming. Human behavior is complex and poorly understood, but there can be no question

that many of the things we do can be explained only in terms of biological impulse. The hormones pumping into our system add confusion to the thoughtless agitation of parents and peers. We sometimes speak of "irrational behavior." We mean that doing such things doesn't make sense. We say, "He wasn't in his right mind." "A thoughtful person would not have behaved in that manner." Or, "Her heart overruled her head." Even the most rational person will do what he is biologically programmed to do whether it makes sense or not. This is one reason children growing up in the same home do not turn out alike. We are born with biological differences that affect attitude, demeanor, and behavior.

Our degree of assertiveness or passiveness is no exception. Some of us are born fighters. Men are generally more violent than women. Women are ordinarily more caring toward infants and children than are men. These may sound like clichés, but they are observable tendencies.

Environment/Hormone Mix

Our genes, of course, do not have the last word. Environment can have overwhelming effects on something like testosterone. Diet, stress, weather, and erotic stimulation all play a part in its production. Hormones affect behavior, but the things we are experiencing influence hormone production.

Men on the Harvard wrestling team were examined with this very question in mind. They all revealed an increase in testosterone level during the fight, but winners had a significantly higher rise than losers. The ones who fought to a draw had levels exactly midway between those of the winners and losers.

Medical science has discovered an undeniable relationship between testosterone levels and human aggression. The higher

4

the level, the earlier the age of the first arrest for juvenile offenders. And yet, differences in behavior between male and female begin long before puberty, when there are not enough sex steroids in the system to make any difference.

There is growing evidence that male and female brains actually have different structures. An experiment with Rhesus monkeys seems to confirm this possibility. Monkeys of both sexes are raised in isolation. They have no sex-role training of any kind. They have no opportunity to identify with a parent of the same sex. When they are about three years old, which compares with a human at about age ten, each monkey is put in a room with a monkey infant. The results show that female juveniles take care of the infant more, and male juveniles hit the infant more. The statistical difference is significant. With no differences in hormone levels, and no differences in the conditions of growing up, there *is* an impressive difference between male and female behavior. Perhaps we should put all of the world's military forces under the control of women! And yet, many men are not aggressive; many women are.

We Fight to Protect Our Territory

Our gender is not the only reason we fight. We also fight to protect what is ours. At the root of much conflict there is nothing more fundamental than personal space, property rights, territory. Children fight loudly over possession of *"my* drum," *"my* swing," or *"my* room."

My family and I once flew from Sarasota, Florida, to Baltimore, Maryland, on discount airfare tickets. People's Express, now out of business, did not assign reserved seats.

While they wouldn't put more people on a plane than it would hold, neither did they bother to organize the boarding process by putting one person in seat 7A and another in 9B. It was "grab it and growl!" I have never been caught in such a chaos of aggression as people charged down the narrow aisle, claiming their respective territories. I wondered what it would be like if we had a fire and all of us had to get out through the tiny exits. Worse, no doubt, than the Three Stooges trying to go through a door.

All God's Creatures Need Space

Finding personal space in a sardine can is not impossible, but our territory there is of poor quality. Crowding destroys social structures. *We need to be a part of a society where we understand and agree upon certain rules for behavior, where we feel included and accepted.* The loss of healthy social ties is behind more drug addiction and suicide than any of us can imagine. It is also at the root of much human aggression.

Traditions, values, and close personal ties tend to disintegrate in a technological society. We may reside in densely populated communities and ride on mass transit facilities, but we feel lonely while being a part of a crowd. A fully populated apartment building or condominium can be a very private place. Sunbelt condo residents sometimes feel lost and isolated. Their experience does not match the dreams inspired in their imagination by the brochures with pictures of palms, sunsets, and happy people. The obvious nearness of other people prevents the sort of pathologies that were fairly common among our Western pioneers, whose nearest neighbor may have been fifty miles away, but the lack of community can be oppressive.

On the other hand, I grew up in a small town where private homes were fairly well scattered and spaced in airy neighborhoods. Even though we had elbowroom we were very much aware of each other. We took mental notes and shared gossip. Few people had any real privacy. Everyone's behavior was on display and reported. This was a significant influence.

A city is overpopulated when it can no longer provide essentials for all of its residents. The essentials, of course, are far more varied than the traditional food, clothing, and shelter. While it is not always helpful to compare the behavior of animals to human behavior, crowded cage studies are revealing. For some species in crowded cages an ample supply of food does not prevent fights. In one case aggressive behavior was actually reduced by cutting the food supply in half. Something else is at play. We need to live in a world fit for humans, where we can know and love each other as persons. When we fight in wars, we learn to call the enemy by names that help us to believe they are not fully human. A slip of the tongue by a soldier being interviewed after Desert Storm is revealing. He said, "We were killing pe—uh, things out there that couldn't see us."

Defense of territory avoids the more serious fighting that would become necessary if the territory were invaded and overcrowded. Most wars begin not in defense of turf, but as a way to grab something desirable. But a nation's leaders cannot gain support for a killing by stating that industry needs less expensive raw materials. The population from which the military is drawn must feel threatened. This is one reason the war in Vietnam was so unpopular. The larger interests of the United States did not seem to be in jeopardy by anything happening in that divided nation.

We Fight in Our Quest for Power

All of us need to feel that we are *in control* of our lives. Many of us have a need to control others. Frankly, we want to be the dominant influence in the largest circle of authority we can manage. In the chicken yard it's called the pecking order.

Sometimes the best we can do is give directions to a passive friend. Or perhaps we dominate a spouse or a child, making all the decisions at home in an autocratic manner. Many of us enjoy positions at work that allow us to boss others around. Professionals, from fields of law enforcement to medical care, experience a sense of controlling power over others. As we will see in a later chapter, this reaches heady, dizzying heights in political and governmental positions. If you can climb high enough up the power pyramid, you can literally get away with murder. (Consider Iraq's Saddam.) Lord Acton, in an 1887 letter to Bishop Creighton, wrote, "Power tends to corrupt and absolute power corrupts absolutely."

When people feel weak and powerless, they will be inclined to strike out. They will fight dirty. They will resort to violence. When we sense that the odds are stacked against us we will feel justified in doing all kinds of underhanded deals. Fighting is the flip side of powerlessness. We will lash out at the person or group that is making us feel helpless.

We need to understand that our drive for personal power is rooted in fear. We are afraid that others will not be able to make good decisions for us. We fear we will lose respect or the sense of being looked up to as a knowledgeable person and a leader.

The Dominance Game

If an animal has become dominant over other animals, it will fight to stay on top. When a human loses status or feels that status is threatened, violent behavior soon follows. Once we have a taste of being in charge, we do not step aside gracefully. Anyone in power wants to stay in power. Anyone subjected to power wants freedom.

Try listening to the conversations going on around you in a public place. You will have little trouble knowing who ranks where in the pecking order. One of the talkers will be brighter or superior in status; another will be less informed. Some will speak in patronizing tones; others will speak loudly. In many ordinary human encounters a subtle effort is made to stay "on top." Soldiers and policemen are trained to play this game effectively, but it also goes on in many offices, athletic fields, and homes.

The Human Difference

Humans are among thousands of species that fight when life-supporting interests are threatened. This is a kind of defensive aggression that stops when the threat is removed. What makes us different from the rest of creation is that we also engage in destructiveness and cruelty. This kind of behavior is not important to our survival, it serves no biological purpose, and it seems to feed some twisted inner desire. This flaw in our nature is probably what has led us to the theological doctrine that we are "fallen creatures." A tiger is not a "sinner" when it bites the throat of its prey. The cat, before she springs, is not angry. A hunter is motivated by different needs than a fighter is. We humans are the only primates who kill and torture our own kind without any clear reason, and who derive some kind of distorted pleasure from it. We are the only sadistic mammal.

Sadism is the term applied to sexual pleasure gained by the infliction of pain or cruelty on others. A sadistic person is hurting inside because he or she is not able to make another person respond in love. Sadism is a way of compensating for this by having power over others.

History shows that human beings are clearly capable of violence that goes far beyond defending ourselves or obtaining life's necessities.

We Fight to Break Up the Boredom

In Shakespeare's play *Coriolanus,* two servants are talking animatedly about an impending battle. One says, "Why then we shall have a stirring world again. This peace is nothing, but to rust iron, increase tailors, and breed ballad makers." The other replies, "Let me have war, say I; it exceeds peace as far as day does night; it's spritely, awaking, audible, and full of vent. Peace is a very apoplexy, lethargy; mulled, death, sleepy, insensible . . ."

General Patton agreed. "I love war," he said.

Sometimes a fight starts simply to stir up a little excitement. Ours is the only species that seems to enjoy destruction without any reason or purpose. We enjoy any kind of exciting stimulation. One of the great differences in people is what it takes to catch attention and bring excitement. I once stood with a man who was moved to tears by the color gradations in a clay bank. I am thrilled by the sound Debussy produces in one of his famous orchestral pieces by having a harp add an attack to each note on the French horn. There are plenty of people who would see and hear mud in both instances.

The plays of Aeschylus, Sophocles, Euripides, Aristophanes, and other classical Greek writers were commercially success-ful when they were first produced. Athenian audiences found them exciting. They were as stimulating to the Greeks as the bloody combat in the Colosseum was to the Romans. But it was a different kind of stimulation.

What Stimulates Us?

Do you have cable TV? Compare one night of AMC with one night of HBO. The American Movie Classics will take you back to a time when films were not rated for sex and vio-lence. The script writer was of primary importance in the production. The current movies running on HBO are some-times clever and well done, but the majority rely upon stunt men, nudity, and spectacular special effects. This indicates a change in our American culture that is clear to anyone with eyesight.

Conflict and bloodshed catch our attention more quickly than scenes of happy families, the wonders of nature, or mental contemplation do. Movie producers have taken note of this and consequently devote more resources and screen time to visual excitement than to quality acting and scripts. Car crashes, gun shots, explosions, fires, and open wounds sell more tickets than conversation and wit do.

One kind of stimulation requires us to be actively involved. Whether it is a movie, some music, a view from a parkway overlook, an idea in print, or another person, our responses are complicated. We have to "get into it." We become participants. Whatever (or whoever) it is we are looking at, listening to, touching, smelling, or tasting is inherently *interesting* to us. It *engages* us. We make discoveries by paying attention. The thing that stimulates us is no longer an "object." We awaken to a new awareness.

The other kind of stimulation demands little effort on our part. It is immediate and direct. We remain passive even when our bodies begin to respond in dance or whatever. We are being driven by basic, primitive excitation of our central nervous system. Eventually the effect wears off, and we no longer respond. This kind of simple stimulation must be increased in intensity or changed in character in order to keep working on us. The short life span of popular music, stylish clothes, elaborate toys, and sex without affection are easy examples of this.

The first kind of stimulation, the activating kind, is never the same experience twice in a row. We develop a relationship with the stimulus that works in both directions. The second kind of stimulation is a trip down a one-way street in someone else's car. This is why someone can listen to one of those long slow movements from a Mahler symphony and never get bored, while another prefers a good foot-stomping beat, without ever noticing it is essentially boring! It is also why one couple can stay faithfully married while another looks for a parade of sexual partners. It takes some growing and maturing to learn patience, concentration, and clear thinking. Emotionally immature people cannot handle frustration or deal with their own greed. They feed on front-page gossip and create conflict of their own. As we will see in chapter 3, some couples stay together precisely because their marriage gives them a way to fight. They seem to need the excitement to stimulate an otherwise boring existence.

Signs of Boredom

A chronically bored person may not realize what is going on. In contemporary America millions of us are bored. We compensate by being very active. We join clubs, take trips to a dozen countries in a dozen days, get lost in sports, and complain about being taxi drivers for our busy children. This great press of activity diminishes our awareness of boredom. The prevailing abuse of drugs begins here, too. Escaping boredom is a powerful impulse.

Fighting is one of the most common antidotes to boredom. Random violence toward innocent victims is one result. "If I stick a knife into that guy, he will react to me." Robbing a bank will certainly break monotony, but it brings with it a risk—the unbearable monotony of life in prison. It is safer to take on our favorite club's recording secretary.

No one is able to live as a meaningless object. The Los Angeles riots of the spring of 1992 were not a new phenomenon, and there will be more to follow. They will happen not only in poverty-stricken ghettos, but in places like prisons and college campuses. We suffer when we are reduced to a number, to a machine that has to be fed and watered. Handouts will not help. Even if we are completely secure and cared for with pampering hands, we crave purpose, adventure—excitement. When these can't be found in high-quality experiences, we can create them for ourselves with acts of destruction.

Young people need strenuous activity. They want their art, films, music, and dance to be vividly intense. The twenty-third Psalm, with its images of green pastures and still waters, is not very appealing. They prefer to dangle from bungee cords or to get in rhythm with flashing strobe lights. A little risk is desirable. Doing something dangerous or struggling against a challenging physical obstacle is living on an important edge. There may well be fewer hazards in the thrills than in unrelieved boredom.

We Fight Because We're Frustrated

Much of our aggressiveness is linked to simple frustration. For instance, a child is taught the demands of society at great personal cost. "Your needs can largely be satisfied, but only at certain times, in particular places, and in specific ways all the rest of us agree on." This kind of frustration is a part of group living. I have been building a little cottage in the woods with my own hands. I want a light bulb in the closet, but the code says I can't have one unless it's battery powered. Somebody somewhere left a regular one on and it started a fire. I don't want scald protection on my shower, but the code says I must have it. People have been seriously burned by hot water. It's frustrating. Systematic frustration of individual desires comes with civilization. As an adult I can cope. I make little adjustments and concessions. But a child can't do that very well.

I was sitting in a corner booth at McDonald's, reading about this very subject when I heard a uniformed clerk cry out, "What did you hit me for?" A little boy, about two years old, had taken a punch at her, a stranger. She looked up at the people with him and said in bewilderment, "I must have done something he didn't like."

Before the American Civil War, black slaves were permitted to be aggressive only toward other slaves. Any open hostility directed toward a white person resulted in extreme punishment. The slaves depended upon their oppressors to keep them alive. Their situation was very similar to that of parent and child. In fact, slaves were spoken to and directed in their tasks as if they were children in adult bodies. The resulting behavior toward their masters showed meek acquiescence and a passive humility. This, of course, concealed a deep and powerful hostility. Many must have "gotten even" in their fantasies.

I was seated at our piano, picking out a new song, when I saw my son, David, reflected in the glass of a framed picture that hung over the music rack. David, who was then about eight, walked up behind me silently, put his hands up beside his ears and began to wag them rapidly in a motion of defiance. He had no idea I could see everything he was doing in the glass over a watercolor.

Psychologists insist that it is unhealthy to repress aggression. It is better to go ahead and express it. All of us have a given amount of aggression to deal with in our own way. What we can't do openly, we do secretly. If we can't punch someone in the nose and get away with it, we will gossip or make slanderous accusations. We might even stick pins in dolls.

The Nature of Aggression

There are many ways to fight without bruising our knuckles. Verbal aggression is widely adopted at home, at work, and at play. We can speak with barely detectable, yet cutting, irony to someone who annoys or offends us. We may tear someone to shreds with words. Sometimes it is an innocent bystander who catches it. We might kick a cat, or a flat tire, or a balky lawn mower. Maybe we curse or swear in public, or defiantly spit on a clean floor. Perhaps we will run a red light or pass on a double line.

Understanding why we fight comes down to understanding *aggressive* behavior, by which we mean action "directed toward others for the purpose of causing injury." The hurt can be either physical or psychological. The word is often misused in common speech. A persistent and assertive salesman is called "aggressive." I saw an ad that spoke of "aggressive" tire tread. But what we are talking about in this book is physical and verbal fighting that inflicts wounds.

Children do things to each other that are illegal in an adult world. But the process is different when we are young. Children fight to keep something important to them—a doll, a blanket, a corner in the sandbox, a candy bar. Children tease each other for the specific purpose of being annoying. Children begin games in the snow and end up going home in tears when it turns rough. Children defend themselves against the provocations of others.

Adult aggressive behavior tends to be criminal. It may stem from a conscious desire to hurt or destroy another person. It may be an impulsive act done in the heat of an emotion like fear or anger. It could be felonious aggression committed in the act of another crime, or as a result of insanity. Some violent aggression is simply *dyssocial,* gaining the approval of a group that considers it the thing to do under the circumstances, such as certain gang activities and initiations.

Modern researchers agree that aggressive behavior has many causes, some of which we are only beginning to recognize. Simple answers are incomplete answers. This introductory chapter has only scratched the surface.

The One Way Out

All of us are trying to make sense of our lives. This is where Christ becomes so important. *We can be changed only as we are converted to a new way of understanding life.* Punishment sometimes "domesticates" us, but only faith can cure us. The person who gets into too many fights is a person who is looking in the wrong places for salvation. Salvation, that venerable church word, comes from the Latin word for "salt" *(sal)*. The idea is that as salt preserves meat from rotting, so Christ can protect us from the destructive forces in ourselves. Fighting, even among unequal combatants, hurts both winner and loser.

The prophet Isaiah gives us a beautiful picture of the peaceable kingdom.

> The wolf will live with the lamb,
>> the leopard will lie down with the goat,
>> the calf and the lion and the yearling together;
>> and a little child will lead them.
> The cow will feed with the bear,
>> their young will lie down together,
>> and the lion will eat straw like the ox.
> The infant will play near the hole of the cobra,
>> and the young child put his hand into the viper's nest.

They will neither harm nor destroy
  on all my holy mountain,
    for the earth will be full of the knowledge of the LORD
    as the waters cover the sea. *Isaiah 11:6-9*

Anyone who has lived long enough to experience the pain and grief of broken relationships, who has suffered vicariously for a loved one or for someone in the news, longs for a world where people can get along with each other without open hostility. This will no more likely evolve in the natural process of human development than that a lion will acquire a taste for straw. Isaiah's vision goes beyond what is natural to what is supernatural. He gives us an image of what only God can do. As we will see in the next chapter, and throughout this book, getting along with others while fulfilling your individual destiny is a gift from God and God alone. We will learn how to apply the insights of Jesus in the complex business of living with others.

2

MAKING UP

A small boy, repeating the Lord's Prayer one evening, prayed: "And forgive us our debts as we
forgive those who are dead against us."
Anonymous

A peculiar feeling from childhood remains etched in
my memory. It was centered somewhere near the
pit of my stomach. It was a physical sensation, but
it was not caused by anything I had eaten or by any illness or
injury. It was entirely emotional.

I had been in an argument with one of my brothers. We
were being loud and angry with each other, and my mother
overheard us and intervened. I don't remember what the struggle was about, but she quickly showed us how ridiculous it
was. As our immature nervous systems calmed down she
said, "Now kiss and make up."

An unpleasant wave of feeling rolled through my abdo-
men. It was like a mixture of nausea and stomachache. Ugh! I
was sorry I had been so argumentative, and I really did love

my brother, but the thought of actually demonstrating how I felt made me ill. From the look on my brother's face, he was equally horrified at the thought.

Making Up Is Not Easy

The English word for restoring friendship and harmony, for resolving conflict and differences, is *reconciliation.* Curiously, it is a term that was put in popular vocabularies by the first generation of Christians. The life, death, and resurrection of Jesus Christ resulted in such a radical change in the religious situation of the earth's people that a new word had to be found to describe it. In the same way our generation has popularized words such as *lifestyle* and *charisma,* first-century Christians seized *reconciliation.* It had been around for a while as an obscure and infrequently used Greek term, but it really came to life in the New Testament.

There is no equivalent for it in Old Testament Hebrew. The *idea* of reconciliation can be found in the Old Testament, but it could be described only in the mending of broken relationships. There was no word that covered the coming to agreement of two or more persons after a misunderstanding.

In religion, the estrangement of people from God was clear enough to the ancient Hebrews. Sinners broke God's laws. They were unfaithful to the covenant. The Jewish sacrificial system provided a way to "atone" for sin, but the world was still waiting for a bridge across the chasm that separated us from our Creator.

This is the work of Jesus Christ. In him, God does for us what we cannot do for ourselves. He *reconciles* us to himself.

The broken relationship is repaired. Paul explains it in the letter he wrote to the Christians in Rome.

> God demonstrates his own love for us in this: While we were still sinners, Christ died for us. Since we have now been justified by his blood, how much more shall we be saved from God's wrath through him! For if, when we were God's enemies, we were reconciled to him through the death of his Son, how much more, having been reconciled, shall we be saved through his life! Not only is this so, but we also rejoice in God through our Lord Jesus Christ, through whom we have now received reconciliation. *Romans 5:8-11*

Reconciliation is a word large enough to hold a lot of thought. So much we have dreamed about and wished for is wrapped up in this single word. It summarizes many volumes of Christian theology. The powerful desire of God; our need; the birth, life, and death of Jesus Christ; and the ministry of the church are all included. Where there was brokenness there is now wholeness. Where there was alienation, there is now reunion. *Reconciliation.* God's power and love reside in it.

Radical News

Paul is telling us that something wildly radical has happened. We are living now in a new age where people can be relieved from the despair of brokenness. The way life used to be is gone. The new has come. And it is God who did it. The reconciliation Paul writes about is not a 50/50 deal. This is not the making up of two friends who have talked out their differences. It is 100 percent God's activity. *We* were lost. *We* were not in a position to negotiate a truce with God. Reconciliation is something God did that fixes the problem.

Writing to the church at Corinth, Paul used his new word to express the concept yet another way.

> If anyone is in Christ, he is a new creation; the old has gone, the new has come! All this is from God, who reconciled us to himself through Christ and gave us the ministry of reconciliation: that God was reconciling the world to himself in Christ, not counting men's sins against them. And he has committed to us the message of reconciliation. We are therefore Christ's ambassadors, as though God were making his appeal through us. We implore you on Christ's behalf: Be reconciled to God.
> *2 Corinthians 5:17-20*

At this point, Paul has "stopped preaching and gone to meddlin'." His fresh word has turned from a theological expression into a guide for daily living. If Christ has reconciled us to God, then the next step is for us to be reconciled to each other; this is a natural progression. The amazing attitude of God toward us needs to be reflected in an equally amazing attitude among God's people. We are to "kiss and make up."

The Teaching of Jesus

Jesus gives us some very practical applications.

> If you are offering your gift at the altar and there remember that your brother has something against you, leave your gift there in front of the altar. First go and be recon-

ciled to your brother; then come and offer your gift.
Matthew 5:23-24

Consciousness of God has a way of stirring the conscience. Nearness to an altar can be very humbling. Whenever I serve communion I am always reminded inwardly of my unworthiness to be handling the sacred bread and cup. My hands feel unclean.

When Jesus indicates that we are likely to remember someone's hard feelings toward us as we bring an offering to the altar he is giving us a little scenario to work out in our imagination. Let's try to reconstruct the scene the way his first hearers would have imagined it.

A page or two ago I said the Jewish sacrificial system was intended to give people a way to atone for their sins. Like most things, it was more complicated than that. The writings of the rabbis make it clear that there is no automatic atonement between sinners and God as a result of ritual sacrifice. Neither, they insist, is there any atonement for offenses between two people—unless they straighten out their difficulties first. The bloody sacrifice had to be accompanied by admission of guilt and some form of penance. The altar is a way to make you better, not a way to excuse yourself. If you are penitent you will honestly try to repair any damage you have done. The idea was clearly that the first order of business was to get right with your neighbor. Only then could you get right with God.

So what would happen? The ancient Jew would have brought his animal offering to the temple to be sacrificed by a priest. He would walk through several public areas, which were used to thin out the crowd and emphasize the seriousness of what was going on. At one point he would pass through a gate designated for Jews only. The Gentiles would be left behind. At another gate he would separate himself from all the Jewish women. Eventually he would be as close as he could get, for only priests were allowed beyond that point. He would wait at this fence until a priest came to receive his sacrificial offering. Now he remembers his argument or bad dealings with another person. For the sacrifice to do what it is intended to do, he is required to go and do everything he can to correct that problem first. See him tying a rope around the rail the way movie cowboys do when they arrive at a saloon. He'll return after he has taken care of something. He walks away, leaving his offering before the altar.

Christians sometimes speak of Christ "hiding" or "covering" their sins. That kind of thinking betrays a misunderstanding of what Christ does for us. It is required of us that *we must do everything in our power to cooperate with God in matters of morality.* The first thing Jesus has to do for us is not to forgive us but to convince us we are sinners. There is no place at the altar for anyone who is at odds with another person. Jesus tells us to go take care of that difficulty immediately. When we do so we will help not only ourselves, but also that other person. If I have made another person angry or sad, I am now involved in that individual's life. We are tied together in this thing. In other words, there are social implications that are far-reaching.

Tradition That Doesn't Pay
Behind everything Jesus teaches in the Sermon on the Mount is the idea that all notions of retaliation, revenge, and hatred are counterproductive.

> You have heard that it was said, "Eye for eye, and tooth
> for tooth." But I tell you, Do not resist an evil person. If
> someone strikes you on the right cheek, turn to him the
> other also. . . . You have heard that it was said, "Love
> your neighbor and hate your enemy." But I tell you: Love
> your enemies and pray for those who persecute you.
> *Matthew 5:38-39, 44*

The ancient Law of the Old Testament permits retaliation in kind.

> But if there is serious injury, you are to take life for life,
> eye for eye, tooth for tooth, hand for hand, foot for foot,
> burn for burn, wound for wound, bruise for bruise.
> *Exodus 21:23-25*

> If anyone injures his neighbor, whatever he has done
> must be done to him: fracture for fracture, eye for eye,
> tooth for tooth. As he has injured the other, so he is to be
> injured. *Leviticus 24:19-20*

> Show no pity: life for life, eye for eye, tooth for tooth,
> hand for hand, foot for foot. *Deuteronomy 19:21*

This law of retaliation remains very much alive in the Middle East both privately and publicly. News often reaches us that a commando attack by one nation was conducted in return for a suicide mission by the other, or that bombs were dropped in retaliation for cannon fire. The sad history of Lebanon is all the proof we need that this kind of exchange sets up a vicious cycle of endless retaliation that settles noth-ing. Situations like that in Northern Ireland assure us that the problem is not limited by geography and culture. For all people everywhere, getting even results in even more hatred and hostility.

Jesus reversed the idea that social order is best preserved by allowing anyone to return evil for evil as long as it is in equal measure. Revenge is a negative principle. We would be mistaken to conclude that Jesus wants us to stand aside and do nothing when we could prevent injury to a helpless person or nation. There are occasions when resisting evil and fight-ing back is the thing demanded of us. Jesus is illustrating a principle. He is not giving us inflexible rules to be interpreted literally in every circumstance.

A New Way

The positive idea Jesus is trying to get us to understand is that we can overcome hatred with love. If we are willing to be insulted, to admit that our critics might have a point, to give more than is required of us, and to be motivated by the requirements of love, things will change. Evil cannot destroy evil; it can only hurt it back. Love has a chance of making a difference. Jesus is offering us the only possible escape from our struggle. This lesson is beautifully stated in the twelfth chapter of Romans: "Do not repay anyone evil for evil. . . . If it is possible, as far as it depends upon you, live at peace with everyone" (verses 17-18).

That may sound like stock morality to you. It is not. Paul is doing far more than simply telling us to be nice to each other. If you read the Roman letter you will see that he has devoted eleven profound chapters to laying a Christian foundation for the ethics he begins to present in chapter 12. He is showing us how to take the love we have seen in Christ and apply it to daily living. Living at peace with everyone is far more than a sweet ideal. It is what is required of anyone who would follow Christ. He is describing a new life in Christ that passes on the kind of love we received from God while we were still God's enemies.

> **Be imitators of God, therefore, as dearly loved children and live a life of love, just as Christ loved us and gave himself up for us as a fragrant offering and sacrifice to God.** *Ephesians 5:1-2*

Love is the essential ingredient in every instance of making up, and "love must be sincere" (Romans 12:9). If you sincerely love others you will bless rather than curse. Love will bind you solidly with all God's creation. This does not come naturally. It is a gift from God. It is one of the things that sets Christian living far apart from the way the secular world conducts its business. It is a reflection of the love seen in Christ. Jesus actually embodied every good behavior Paul describes in his lesson on living as part of the Christian community. The Gospels show us a Jesus who is the perfect example of patience, kindness, peacefulness, gentleness, self-control, and love. He is not merely keeping his cool by not getting involved. He becomes passionately involved. He demonstrates how to love an enemy. He shows us how to pray for those who persecute us. "When they hurled their insults at him, he did not retaliate; when he suffered, he made no threats" (1 Peter 2:23). In Jesus we see the incarnation of a new kind of love, and we begin to understand that hating an enemy only reinforces the separation.

Practical Application That Works

Let's be realistic. I know a young woman who honestly tries to love others in a completely open, caring, idealistic way. She lives in one of our nation's largest cities. Because she has suffered personal injury at the hands of aggressive people in the inner city she has had to learn to be "street smart" to survive. But this does not invalidate her desire to love everyone and anyone. It shows the divine wisdom that inspired Paul to add the phrase "as far as it depends upon you."

In the chapters that follow we will look at some specific challenges to living at peace with everyone. The guidance you will find in these pages is Christianity at its most practical. There are realistic and honestly helpful ways of applying Christ's teaching in the daily business of living and earning a living. We need to be reminded of them. Can we ever forget Rodney King's horrified and bewildered expression in the wake of the Los Angeles riots? "Hey," he stammered, searching for any words that would coherently express his horror, "Can't we get along?"

3

FAMILY SQUABBLES

It is a reverent thing to see an ancient castle or building not in decay: or to see a fair timber tree sound and perfect. How much more to behold an ancient and noble family which hath stood against the waves and weathers of time.

Sir Francis Bacon

I received a long distance call from a member of a church I had served more than a decade ago. The woman was in tears. She said she had not slept for days. The problem was that her son, a grown man, could not get along with his father. As a result, she could not see her grandchild in her own home. Her husband was openly disappointed in their son's achievements in life. The caller felt caught in the middle. She wanted to help, but she could not think of anything to do. She said she had been praying about the problem for a long time and was desperate. It was beginning to affect her health.

"Do you think it would do any good if I told my son how this is working on me?"

"You mean he doesn't know?" I asked.

"No, I have tried to hide it from him. You know, I want to be supportive."

Family Strife Is Inevitable

Close living naturally breeds conflict. Whenever two or more people occupy the same space for an extended period of time there are going to be disagreements and contests. Rivalry is perfectly normal; it's not supposed to be any other way. And there is nothing anyone can do to avoid it. The important thing is to keep it under control, to let it work in a healthy way. If it gets out of hand, it becomes destructive.

Home can be a dangerous place. Domestic violence is the source of most police statistics on shootings, stabbings, and assaults. Whether it happens in the house, on the street, or at the bar, most of the combatants know each other intimately.

What you are reading now does not address this kind of violence. A stronger family member beating up a weaker family member is simply wrong. Psychological abuse by a more sophisticated family member is no less reprehensible. If marks are being left on flesh, if wounds to the spirit are deep, painful, and permanent, things have gone haywire. You need the police, the courts, and professional counseling to help you untangle such a mess. The family squabbles we are trying to deal with in these pages have not yet come to blows.

The normal conflict that comes along with living together in families can be helpful rather than damaging. When one person complains about the unreasonableness of the demands being placed upon him, this indicates growth on his part—a growing consciousness of selfhood. Whether anything is gained or not, growth has taken place. Every time some point of conflict arises, the people involved have the opportunity to develop further in character and maturity. There is no way this kind of disagreement can be bad. Children especially need to test how much they can get away with. Parents have the responsibility to set limits and then adhere to them consistently. Every child is forever pushing at behavioral walls and doors, looking for ways to enlarge the territory his or her personality can occupy. It is through this kind of probing and experimentation that we define who we are. "Fighting," in this sense, is a necessary part of human development. A first step in healthy family life is to put away expectations that "good families don't fight."

A healthy family fight does not have as its goal the injuring of another person. It involves give and take. Home provides a fairly comfortable and secure place where we can go ahead and say the unsayable and ask the unaskable. Instead of trying to avoid conflict, healthy families get it out in the open and deal with it. This takes some practice, skill, and a lot of patience. Someone needs to referee. With as little emotional involvement as possible, a third person needs to listen to both sides with objectivity. This parent or child can step in when necessary and encourage understanding rather than the escalating of emotion.

Hazards to Avoid

A quarrel or dispute that is not quickly mended can go on breeding worse trouble as time goes by. Bitterness breeds bitterness. A disagreement between two people can extend to *their* families so that the fight goes on for generations.

I began my ministry in the Appalachian Mountains, an area notorious for its family feuds. I thought the legend of the Hatfields and the McCoys was a quaint bit of pioneer history. I was surprised to discover that this was a pattern of family relationships that still continues in isolated instances. I was talking about this with a young woman in the area who had recently earned a college degree. I expressed my horror that such hostility could go on for so long.

"Oh," she said, "we're having a feud right now in one part of my family! We haven't spoken to them for several years." I looked at her in astonishment. She was an intelligent woman, dressed in modern clothes. I asked if there were any reasons for this feeling she shared with her side of the family.

"Yes, of course there's a reason. It's not much of one and both sides are responsible. I don't hold anything against them personally."

"Then you would talk to them?"

"Oh, no! I could be in the same room with them and not even *see* them!"

If at the very beginning of a family dispute one of the parties can find the grace to apologize or admit fault, a wasteful and sometimes deadly situation will never have to come about. Get to work on it. In most situations prompt action will bring healing. Healing is *much* easier in the beginning; ignore the wound, and it will become a festering sore. The bitterness will spread to other areas—even other people.

The country preacher who married Anna and me gave us this bit of advice: "Don't go to bed mad." That is a variation on the Bible's "Do not let the sun go down while you are still angry" (Ephesians 4:26).

That's a beautiful saying, but it has its dangers at home. If the only way you can go to sleep in peace is to give in to a more dominant person, you have not reached an agreement. You have surrendered. If one personality must cave in to another personality, the family is losing its tolerance of individuality. We can live together without denying the differences that distinguish one individual from another.

An Example to Study

Let me create a fictional family squabble for us to analyze. It is not entirely accurate to call it fiction because it is a composite of many situations that have been brought into my study by tearful family members. There is nothing in my little scenario that does not go on all the time in the world we live in every day.

Kim was thrilled to be old enough to get her driver's license. She asked for the keys to the family car one Saturday so she could take some friends for a ride. Mom explained that she needed the car to go to the supermarket. She had agreed to bake a cake that night for a church picnic on Sunday and needed to buy the ingredients.

"I'll pick them up for you," Kim offered.

Mom took her up on it. "OK. Here's ten dollars. Pick up a yellow cake mix, some chocolate frosting, and a gallon of milk."

Kim took the ten dollar bill, the keys to the car, and fairly skipped out of the house in happiness.

Now that she had an errand runner in the family, Mom discovered a new freedom. Instead of another trip to the store, she could walk down the block and visit some neighbors.

Later that evening, when she was ready to bake the cake, she could not find the supplies. She walked into the hall, where Kim was in deep conversation on the telephone, and asked where she put the grocery bag.

Her daughter cupped her hand over the phone, shrugged her shoulders, and said, "I forgot!" Her facial expression conveyed such an apologetic message Mom struggled to conceal her disappointment. Kim spoke a few words to her friend on the other end of the line.

"Well, give me the ten dollars and I'll get it now before they close."

Kim was lost in her conversation and did not respond.

"Give me the money so I can go get it!"

At that, Kim looked up startled. "I don't have it."

"Where is it?"

"I spent it on gas and hamburgers."

"Kim!" Mom exploded, "hang up that phone right now!" She suddenly unleashed a tirade against her daughter, calling her into account for all of her irresponsible behavior over the years. There was the day she didn't mail the electric bill, the time she failed to wash the dishes, the mess in her room, on and on, with feeling.

The daughter, wanting to spare her friend at the other end of the line all of this outburst, quickly spoke into the phone, "I'll call you back," and hung up. When her mother paused for a breath she jumped in with a protest of her own. "You're not perfect! You ought to take a look at yourself! All you can do is complain about everybody else around here. You have

34

embarrassed me in front of my best friend!" Kim's face turned red with anger.

"Just for that, young lady, you won't get to use the car for six months!" Mom's chin was quivering with emotion. "You are grounded!"

At this point Dad arrives. He heard the yelling from out on the back porch and wants to know what is going on. The fussing between the two women continues in his presence. He touches his wife's elbow. "Hey, give the kid a break."

She turns to him in rage. "This is between us, so you can just stay out of this, mister! You're always taking her side. That's why she's so defiant. You don't know what a mess she's gotten me into. There is no way I will be able to take a cake to the picnic tomorrow. I'll have to take the blame for her irresponsibility. You've spoiled her since she was a little girl!"

Stung, Dad flushes a little in the face himself. His calm, confident voice is replaced with one that becomes more strident with each vowel. "You let me know when you can listen to reason! I'm going back out on the porch!"

They watch him storm away, slamming the door behind him.

Why do things like this happen? Because they follow a very good set of rules for a typical family squabble:

- Begin with any problem (the missing cake mix).

- Expand the field (mail, dishes, messy room, etc.).

- Return some good shots in self-defense ("You're not perfect," and "You're embarrassing me").

- Get in the last word (no car for six months).

- Affirm the impossibility of change ("You always take her side"; "She's spoiled").

- Get away from the issues and into personalities (all of the above).

- Eliminate any escape hatch for bargaining room (you're grounded).

- Draw in new personalities (Dad comes in from the porch).

- Walk away before there can be resolution (doorslam).

A real problem in the intimacy of strife at home is that we do not think about guarding our tongue. We go ahead and say whatever has boiled to the surface by the heat of the fight. We trap ourselves in verbal sinkholes. When our three children spaced two years apart were young, tension and tears were not uncommon. I remember one hot summer afternoon when battle fatigue set in. Our verbal exchanges had not achieved the desired solutions. Caught up in this battle spirit, I impulsively said to Anna, "I don't think I want to go with you to the art show this afternoon." With equal spontaneity she shot back, "Good!" I was shattered. That wasn't where I wanted this thing to go. We were trapped by our own hasty mouths, saying things neither of us actually meant.

The Position of Scripture

The Bible takes a very clear stand on all human relationships. In every situation it consistently favors reconciliation over separation. Regarding marriage and family life, the sacred pages plead with us to get along. Stable, enduring relationships are presented as the only way to human health and happiness.

> To the married I give this command (not I, but the Lord): A wife must not separate from her husband. But if she does, she must remain unmarried or else be reconciled to her husband. And a husband must not divorce his wife. *1 Corinthians 7:10-11*

> Clothe yourselves with compassion, kindness, humility, gentleness and patience. Bear with each other and forgive whatever grievances you may have against one another. Forgive as the Lord forgave you. And over all these virtues put on love, which binds them all together in perfect unity. . . .
> Wives, submit to your husbands, as is fitting in the Lord.
> Husbands, love your wives and do not be harsh with them.
> Children, obey your parents in everything, for this pleases the Lord.
> Fathers, do not embitter your children, or they will become discouraged. *Colossians 3:12-14, 18-21*

Everyone needs forgiveness. It is not a matter, says Paul, of putting up with others, but rather of bearing with each other. The question of whether Christian behavior is "manly" or "womanly" is simply irrelevant. When you are at home, boys, girls, husbands, wives, do your part to get along with each other. Family structures are overdue for healthy changes. While it is troubling to see how poorly some of the experimental attempts at change (such as wife swapping) are working out, it is a joy to see the new awakening in our day to the best possibilities for family life. The important consideration is whether people are being helped or hurt by any new arrangement at home. If children are being emotionally injured, if adults are stressed beyond belief, then there must be a better way.

The people who first read Paul's list of home responsibilities lived in a society quite different from our own. But the responsibility of applying the spirit of Christ to our home life has not diminished in any way. The rules laid down in the New Testament are not specific. They speak in a general way about living in Christian harmony. Families that seek the influence of God tend to be more successful in reconciling their differences. Not always—even the gospel includes a loophole of adultery in its prohibition of divorce. But generally speaking, family life goes better with God than without God.

Jesus encountered many people during his brief ministry. It is recorded in the New Testament that he improved their lives whenever they would let him. He knew how to get to the bottom of an issue. He was a problem solver. He continues to help modern families resolve their difficulties. With Christ's love, it is possible to end conflict at home and solidify family relationships. There are six steps any family can follow.

- *Identify the problem.* This may not be easy. Embarrassing situations are hard to face. Misleading symptoms can mask reality. Nagging and complaining are never the basic problem. Even financial difficulties are sometimes only a cover for something else. Males tend to be the most hesitant to openly state the essential problem. There will be no reconciliation until you are fixing the right thing.

- *Look for alternative solutions.* Let everyone speak. How can this problem be reduced or eliminated? Does your proposal rely upon everyone else but you? Think about your preconceived solution. Is there another way? Try to avoid open reaction to the comments of others even if you find them exasperating. Determine in advance that everyone will remain open and neutral as ideas are shared. Anything less will bring another explosion of profitless emotion.

- *Agree on the best alternative.* By this point you should have a wide range of potential solutions to your difficulty. Try each one out in your imagination. Some may seem complex and difficult. Others will be simple and direct. Which one is best? What are the pros and cons? It is probable that none of the solutions will be without a down side. Which one has the highest ratio of positives? Allow some time to think it over. Try to reach some kind of consensus.

- *Get to work on it now.* Agreeing on a solution is a giant step, but implementation will not follow automatically. Every participant is responsible for making it happen. If reconciliation depends upon changing some long-standing habits, don't expect instant miracles. Deep changes of this kind come gradually. New patterns of behavior have to be learned.

- *Rebuild the relationship.* Don't let anyone feel that he or she has "lost." Choosing the best alternative probably means that ideas of others have been discarded. This can be a downer. If anyone is a clear "winner," let that person show nothing but love and support for the others—no victory celebrations. This is where my mother's advice about kissing and making up is nothing less than pure wisdom. Do some hugging. Touch can be life giving. Maybe you can see each other differently now.

- *Review what you have done.* If the struggle has been intense, it can be helpful to look back over the progress you have made. If each step so far has been pleasing, imagine how much better things will be if you continue. Thank God together for your growth as a maturing family.

An Example from Real Life

You can go home again if you have changed and do not expect the other members of your family to be changed. The change in you may well elicit changes in others.

A couple, married for fifty years, produced a yellowing sheet of paper that had been folded and tucked aside long ago. They had experienced a serious tiff. Verbally, she had threatened to leave him. That painful possibility carried with it the shattering of a beautiful relationship that had little hope of ever being repaired. In anger he had replied, "All right, but if you do, don't ever come back!" People say things like that to each other when they are under stress and can't see an escape route. It is not much different from the child's emotional outburst to a frustrating parent: "I wish you were dead!"

After things had cooled off, she wrote down her response. So significant that it has been preserved all these years, this piece of paper has only four sentences, but they define her part in a living relationship. (Looking at it is a little like violating a private sanctuary, but I have their permission to print it.)

> "I don't know now what is true and right, but it doesn't matter. You are the reason I live and if you want me docile or however, I'll try to be. I'm promising myself and God. If I slip, forgive me and I'll try again."

She drew a little heart as a seal.

That may not be an answer for everyone, but it has worked for these two very talented and creative people. Take a close look at what she says.

"I don't know now what is true and right . . ." She has conceded nothing, but she has left the door open to the possibility that her husband has a point worth considering. A few hours before only she was right.

". . . but it doesn't matter." Being right or wrong is not as important as our relationship.

In fact, "You are the reason I live . . ." When people are in love and truly committed to each other, there is no independent life worth living. One life gives the other life meaning. One blade of a pair of scissors can be used for sticking and gouging, but the two together fulfill a larger and more useful purpose.

". . . and if you want me docile or however, I'll try to be." That may disturb you. A docile wife is a wife filled with hidden resentments. When I marry a couple I never ask the bride to promise to "love, honor, and obey" her husband. In the weddings I conduct the vows are identical for both parties. I don't call that 50/50. I call it 100/100! And yet, look at her honesty. Her statement can be interpreted: "I sense you need me to be a little more flexible. I recognize you have peculiar requirements of your own because of who you are. For the sake of our love, I will attempt to be the kind of partner you can live with best. I can't promise you this. But I promise to try."

"I'm promising myself and God." My promise is not to you. I have too much healthy self-identity for that. I would have to throw myself away to be exactly what you think you want all the time. You fell in love with me the way I am. I don't believe you really want me to be someone else, or no one at all. I have an inner resolve to work at this thing, to keep your needs in mind. It is a private, spiritual thing. I believe it is pleasing in God's sight. With God as my partner in this I will more likely be able to pull it off. It won't be easy. I will need God's help. But I have promised myself and God that I will try.

"If I slip . . . " I probably will. Maybe I should have said, "When I slip . . . "

" . . . forgive me . . . " It is going to cost the husband. He will have to accept less than a perfect wife. For the relationship to work a burden of patience and pardon will be on you even as it is certainly on me.

" . . . and I'll try again." This is an open-ended, living agreement. None of that ill-considered one-way-trip, wish-you-were-dead stuff tossed off by passionate youth. It is a mature, continually renewable, conscious effort on the part of both of us.

I don't know if she showed him this at the time of their struggle or not. It may have been a private thing, written and tucked away like a prayer in Jerusalem's Wailing Wall. There can be no question that it was a pivotal moment for both of them. It has worked, and it continues to work. We can learn from them.

If family strife is your major concern, don't stop reading because you have reached the end of this chapter. The principles of conflict-resolution and negotiation that follow in other chapters will be equally helpful at home.

4

NEIGHBORLY DISPUTES

Deal with another as you'd have
Another deal with you;
What you're unwilling to receive,
Be sure you never do.
The New England Primer

My brother-in-law was mowing his lawn. The blade picked up a small stone and hurled it over onto his neighbor's patio. His neighbor screamed angrily, "I'm going to sue you!"

Times are changing. The difference in "neighborliness" during my brief lifetime came into sharp focus on opening day of trout season. The stream was stocked with state hatchery trout that have all the fight and taste of wet newspaper, but its banks were lined with a swarm of eager fishermen. Men, women, and children bristled with newly purchased gear. A few looked as though they had stepped right out of a calendar picture with hip boots, net, creel, and a hat peppered with artificial lures they would never use. They may have been fantasizing about standing alone in a crystal clear pool at the bottom of a remote waterfall, but they were in a carnival.

The fish were supposed to bite anything that resembled the pellets they had been reared on—salmon eggs, corn, etc. But something was wrong that Saturday. The action was slow.

When a man who had escaped the crowd by wading out to stand on a rock in midstream reeled in a respectable rainbow trout, the most remarkable thing happened. Many of the people on the banks around him, after witnessing his good fortune, sprang into the water. Frantically they jostled and shoved as they scrambled for a piece of that best place to be. The man who had caught the trout was actually pushed off the rock the way children play "King of the Mountain." In less than a minute and a half after the iridescent sides of the rainbow were exposed to air, there was a total snarl of fishing lines, elbows, and voices. Any trout in the area surely moved on to quieter waters.

I remember how it was when my Dad took me fishing on the freshwater lakes near our home. From the time I was old enough to hold a bamboo pole until I went away to college, we went fishing about once a week except in the bitterest winter weather. This special time with him was one of the great assets of my life. I learned a lot about fishing, information I no longer use. I learned a lot more about living, lessons I apply every day.

We fished from lightweight, blunt-ended, wooden boats with a unique "well" near the middle that would keep our catch alive. No outboard motors were permitted even though

Lake Kilby was fairly large. We paddled silently and slowly from one favorite spot to another. If we approached another boat, Dad would guide us far around it in order not to disturb the fishermen. At a distance of fifty to seventy-five feet he would call out, "Having any luck?" The reply would always be a soft, "No. Not doin' much today."

We fished the area so often we had a fairly good idea which places were likely to be productive. One or two locations were nearly always worth fishing, and we would turn to them when all the others let us down. After a particularly poor day, when we were going to return home empty-handed, we decided to go to one of those "smokehouses." As we approached, a lone fisherman was tied to our tree limb, pulling in our fish, one after another.

"Come on," I said, "let's catch some fish!"

Dad stopped paddling, a desperate yet resigned expression on his face. "No," he said. "He got here first." He steered the familiar arc around the other boat. "Any luck?"

"Not much," the man replied, putting fresh bait on his hook. "Not a very good day today."

The Meaning Behind the Law

The secret to being a good neighbor is neither complicated nor difficult. Jesus told us how to do it: Be considerate of others. It's that simple. All the complexity of law and regulation have a common root.

> The commandments, "Do not commit adultery," "Do not murder," "Do not steal," "Do not covet," and whatever

47

other commandment there may be, are summed up in this one rule: "Love your neighbor as yourself." *Romans 13:9*

All the commandments in the Bible and nearly every law passed by Congress, state, and local legislatures mean essentially one thing. Care about others. Love them in the way that Christians mean when they speak of *agapē*. *If all we are conscious of are the various laws that restrict our behavior, we are missing the hidden unity behind them all*. Legalism sees only the rules and regulations. In fact, all religious and civil laws have one essential thing to declare: *Respect your neighbor's rights*. Each law is an individual example of how this larger principle may be applied. If we truly loved our neighbor, there would be no further need of any law. "Love *(agapē)* does no harm to its neighbor. Therefore love *(agapē)* is the fulfillment of the law" (Romans 13:10). Everything the law demands would already be done.

I live in the same world you do. "Mr. Rogers' Neighborhood," where everyone is so gentle, helpful, and friendly, exists only on TV screens. Obviously, the commandment to love our neighbor as ourselves is not widely practiced. "Love your neighbor, but be careful of your neighborhood" is good advice. Even in Christ's time there were those who tried to escape the pressures of the injunction by asking for a precise definition of *neighbor*. It would be a little easier, maybe, if that could be an exclusive term. The parable of the Good Samaritan is our Lord's answer. He leaves no doubt that all the world is one neighborhood. We can't control who our neighbors are. They will decide how they are going to behave. The only thing we have the power to govern is our own pattern of living. Our job is to be good neighbors. Sometimes this will make the critical difference. Sometimes it will not. Either way we will have been faithful to the injunction to live peaceably with others as far as it depends upon us.

Becoming Neighborly

Common wisdom says, "You've got to be a neighbor to have one." Sometimes we overlook the simplest ways to do considerable good. We pass up opportunity after golden opportunity to make some very practical applications of Christ's teaching.

Being a neighbor is not all that difficult. I know what you want to tell me: "You don't know my neighbors." But I do. I live with them just like you do. Some of the most challenging neighbors I have ever dwelt among were in a beautiful neighborhood on Florida's Gulf Coast. I don't know what the problem was. Perhaps it was the rootlessness we all experienced. Maybe it was the heat and humidity. It could have been something in me. Like every neighborhood, it was a mixture of all kinds of people. Many were dear souls, extroverted and warm. Some stayed out of sight, driving into their garages, automatically closing the door, and barricading themselves from whatever stirred outdoors. A few were aggressive and hostile, arguing over the placement of trash cans by the curb, height of fences, lawn mowing frequency, and such. And of course there were plenty of adolescents working off excess energy with randomly or specifically directed hostility.

Quiet, Please!

Even in a community where I did not feel particularly at home, there were plenty of opportunities to learn about being a neighbor. For example, what could be more basic than respecting the rights of others to quiet? I did not rev up a car engine at odd hours of the night or blast loud music through my windows. But since ours was the only home in the neighborhood without a little pool in the back yard, we did have one put in for the children.

Unfortunately, the water table on the coast of Florida is only a foot or two below the surface. When a hole is dug for a pool it soon fills with ground water. In the rainy season, an empty pool will rise up and float like a ship. The only way to deal with this is for the construction crew to use a gasoline powered machine called a wet hog. It pumps water from the excavation twenty-four hours a day. A wet hog is an extraordinarily irritating necessity. It is *loud*. The continually running engine sounds like a large lawnmower. This is mixed with the *slurp, gronk, splat* of the water-sucking mechanism.

It takes awhile to get even a modest pool in the ground. Day after day, night after night, the wet hog churned and groaned and sputtered. When the workmen finally turned it off, there was applause from an invisible audience behind fences all over the block. The only comforting fact was that every one of them had also used wet hogs.

When we moved from Florida we bought a home on a heavily wooded lot in Virginia. Other houses were all around us, but most of them were out of sight beyond the dense growth of trees. I became an enthusiastic home gardener, clearing junky areas and planting ornamentals. Soon I had a gigantic pile of brush. A friend gave me a vintage shredder that enabled me to turn that brush pile into mulch. All I had to do one spring Saturday was pull the rope on the five-horsepower engine, bring it up to speed, and feed in the material. It was slow work, but it was fun.

It was also noisy. Shredders make a special kind of wail as they grind from the thick end of a limb to the finer branches at the tip. Standing close to it, I resorted to hearing protectors. When I finished the job at day's end, cut off the engine, and let the thing wind down, the same phenomenon I had observed in Florida took place. There was applause all around me from positions out of sight beyond the trees.

Noise pollution is demonstrably hazardous to human health. An easy place to begin being a good neighbor is by being a little quieter. Think about other people. You may be enjoying your tape deck in your car or your radio at the beach, but others may not share your taste and enthusiasm. You may be having a good time telling a story to your friends in the restaurant, but others may be getting indigestion. You may prefer to mow your lawn before the sun gets too high, but someone else may need to sleep. It doesn't take much effort to soften the edges of your audible aura. All you have to do is start being conscious that others are out there.

It Takes Common Sense

It doesn't take a powerhouse of a brain to think of dozens of ways to love our neighbors as ourselves. Dogs are popular pets. They are affectionate, appreciative, obedient, sometimes cuddly, often protective, and usually considered members of the family. They also invade other people's territory. Many bark at strangers, attacking them if they can. In the worst cases they maim and kill. Mild-mannered dogs roam the neighborhood marking almost anything vertical with their scent. They do a lot of what the British call "fouling the footpath." Dogs make messes on neighbors' lawns. It is not pleasant to step into fresh dog droppings while picking up the morning newspaper. Controlling a pet is another basic step toward becoming a good neighbor.

But suppose the problem is your neighbor's dog? How you respond is an issue of neighborliness also. Much will depend upon how persistent the problem is, and the kind of response you have received in the past. If you are exasperated, you may threaten the dog (or its owner) with death, or some less idiotic retaliation. Threats will not get you very far. They don't repair damage; they make things worse. Threats bring on a wild kind of confusion. They do not bring the peace you seek. If the dog's owner thinks you are so upset that you might actually carry out your threat, you may hear from the police. The division will grow wider.

It is perfectly understandable that you have a right to defend yourself. Restraining the aggression of others is often necessary. Christ does not require us to be weak or passive. The point is that threats and violence are destructive. Reconciliation occurs when neighbors enter into an agreement to try to solve a problem with mature judgment. Rather than avoiding the other party, open doors to friendship and negotiation. Patience is an important virtue.

"You don't know my neighbors."

Do you mean it doesn't pay to be nice, considerate, hospitable, friendly, unselfish, cooperative, courteous, or neighborly? Do those words seem horribly outdated, something like the thing Boy Scouts used to say?

"You don't know my neighbors."

It is easier to decide your neighbor is a louse than to start the kind of conversation that may lead you to change your mind. If you are in luck, maybe some of them will eventually move. But there is a better way, one that depends largely on you. It is not guaranteed to turn an old grouch into a pleasant companion. It will not make a violence-prone individual any less threatening. (See chapter 11 on the ones you will probably lose.) But in most instances, you have a choice of better and poorer ways to resolve neighborly disputes.

Living in Close Proximity

The neighborhood where you live is a microscopic example of the larger community of the world. Life together can be healthy and productive, or it can be sick and destructive. For good things to happen, it is usually necessary for neighbors to desire it and work together for it to happen. In the same way that marriage involves active effort by both spouses to make it work, neighbors get along better when they work at it. Hostility and aggression are powerful obstacles to the formation of creatively constructive communities. In this kind of atmosphere valuable energy gets misdirected. In some groups of people there is a definite limit how much rivalry and animosity can be absorbed before serious damage is being done.

We have developed courts and other institutions to deal with our conflicts. Cultures other than our own have come up with a variety of ways to settle differences between neighbors that fall short of violence and bloodshed. These can be amusing in their simplicity and originality. In what we mistakenly refer to as "primitive cultures," disputes between two people have a way of spreading through the community as neighbors take sides. It is important for the welfare of the community for these conflicts to be stopped as quickly as possible. Sometimes an older, wiser person will intervene in an unbiased manner. It is possible that one of the individuals is clearly in the right, or it may be only a question of popularity. In these instances the public may judge the merits of the case as a common opinion becomes known to the combatants.

If these easy steps do not solve the issue, societies that are held together in bands in wilderness areas tend to call for some kind of open contest. A game is better than a battle. Perhaps it will be a wrestling match. Some tribes practice head-butting. (So do some church committees!) The fight takes place in public, and the winner is declared to have won his case.

Have you ever heard of Eskimo song duels? The weapons are words set to music. They use little, sharp words, like splinters, to work off grudges and disagreements. In East Greenland, I am told, the Eskimos can become so engrossed in the artistry of singing that they forget the cause of the grudge. Like boxers, they have devised a highly conventionalized way in which to fight. There are traditional patterns of song composition. The winner will deliver his music with such finesse as to elicit the most applause from the audience. He goes home with prestige, while the loser is derided with laughter. The decision of the community is clear. Primitive? Maybe not. When I called our local reference librarian for help in locating some facts about song duels she said, "I wish we could all do that."

Becoming a good neighbor requires a high degree of honesty, integrity, and unselfishness. Agreeing where property boundaries are is a good way to prevent hard feelings. Is the tree you want to cut down actually on your land? Have you stacked your firewood on your side of the line? That this is an ancient source of contention is indicated by the Old Testament's warning, "Cursed is the man who moves his neighbor's boundary stone" (Deuteronomy 27:17).

As Christ's Good Samaritan assures us, we have neighbors who don't live next door. The requirements of being a good neighbor extend to everyone who is affected by our personal decisions.

When Jesus was passing through Jericho he had an encounter with the local tax collector, Zacchaeus, who had grown wealthy at the expense of his neighbors. In the same way that turn-of-the-century circus ticket salesmen earned a living by shortchanging yokels, the Roman system of taxation allowed tax collectors to make a profit by taking in all they could above what was expected by the government. It was a lucrative appointment. The people, of course, could see what was going on. Zacchaeus was, to put it mildly, *not* a popular person. As a Jew, his association with the Roman government was in itself enough to cause him to be ostracized. Add to this his luxurious living at his neighbor's expense, and you can begin to understand the degree to which he would have been disliked.

Luke tells us Zacchaeus was a short man, and because of the crowd that had gathered beside the road to see Jesus pass by he could not get a view. With a little imagination we can see his neighbors intentionally crowding him out. Running ahead of the action, Zacchaeus climbed a sycamore tree that branched out over the road. It was from that elevated position that he caught Jesus' eye. With divine insight Jesus invited Zacchaeus to come down and have lunch with him. The people were astonished, indignant.

> But Zacchaeus stood up and said to the Lord, "Look, Lord! Here and now I give half of my possessions to the poor, and if I have cheated anybody out of anything, I will pay back four times the amount." *Luke 19:8*

Jesus has a way of reconciling neighbors that often involves heavy participation by the one who is "in the right." Easing tensions and resolving neighborly disputes may mean you have to give rather than receive. Look at it this way: the person who is more in the right is really more free *emotionally* to be generous. The troublemaker is often the one saddled with guilt or feeling backed into a corner; he or she will find it more difficult to give in, which means that the greater part of giving often rests on the shoulders of the least offender. Is it really that important to be declared right? Much of the time being at peace is the better option. Don't fret over this too much; Jesus said that givers are more blessed than receivers.

I once heard a charming story about Abraham Lincoln. It may be apocryphal or it could be true. Either way, it is worth passing on. When Lincoln was practicing law in Fulton and Menard counties in Illinois, he rode a horse that was somewhat past prime. It was a ragged nag, patient and plodding, but it got Abe and his saddlebags of books where he was going.

On his way to Lewiston, Lincoln met a gentleman he knew.

"Hello, Uncle Tommy."

"Hello, Abe. I'm powerful glad to see ye, fer I'm goin' to have somethin' fer ye at Lewiston court, I reckon."

"How's that, Uncle Tommy?"

"Well, Jim Adams, his land runs 'long o' mine. He's pesterin' me a heap, an I got to get the law on him, I reckon."

"Uncle Tommy, have you had any fights with Jim?"

"No."

"He's a fair to middlin' neighbor, isn't he?"

"Only tol'able, Abe."

"He's been a neighbor of yours for a long time, hasn't he?"

"Nigh on to fifteen year."

"Part of the time you get along all right, don't you?"

"I reckon we do, Abe."

"Well now, Uncle Tommy. You see this horse of mine? He isn't as good a horse as I could straddle, and I sometimes get out of patience with him, but I know his faults. He does fairly well as horses go, and it might take me a long time to get used to some other horse's faults. All horses have faults. You and Uncle Jimmy must put up with each other as I and my horse do with one another."

"I reckon, Abe," said Uncle Tommy, biting off a chew of tobacco, "I reckon you are about right."

A smile came to Abe Lincoln's gaunt face as he rode on toward Lewiston.

May we be as wise as Abe and Uncle Tommy in our actions toward our neighbors.

5

OVERCOMING PREJUDICE

I never read a book before reviewing it;
it prejudices a man so.
Rev. Sydney Smith (1771–1845)

Long ago, the prophet Malachi asked two vitally important questions. "Have we not all one Father? Did not one God create us?" (Malachi 2:10). This issue is coming to a climax in our time. The survival of civilization depends upon how we answer. Do we honestly believe we are all God's children? Is there only one human race with a common destiny? Or is it true, after all, that it comes down to "them and us"? Are we one world of people, or are we a great number of races, tribes, and nations who must fight with each other until the winner takes all?

Christianity has always taught that there is one God who is the Creator and Sustainer of us all, regardless of our observable differences. Christianity's goal is a saved world and the reconciliation of all people everywhere—not only to God, but also to each other.

The *Declaration of Independence* holds that all men are created equal. There is no verse of Scripture that teaches this. Obviously, we are all quite unequal in our natural resources. Some of us are strong; others are weak. Some have many talents, others have few. Our mental capacities span a remarkably wide area. Health is distributed with a terrible inequality. Christianity teaches something that goes far beyond Thomas Jefferson's famous statement. Many consider it outrageous. We believe that in spite of all our differences we remain *equal before God.* God is concerned about all of us equally, in the same way that a good parent cares for every child regardless of how many may be in the family and which one is the greatest achiever. "God does not show favoritism" (Acts 10:34). In fact, if God has any greater interest in anyone it is reserved for those who are weak, burdened, and outcast.

Tolerance levels in American society are slowly increasing, but there are not many of us who are free from prejudice. Nearly all of us are down on something or someone. I remember a lady who said, "I look down on people who look down on people." The time may have come for us to examine our personal prejudices and perhaps to overcome some of them.

A Definition of Terms

We need to begin by being sure we understand what we mean when we use two popular words: *prejudice* and *discrimination.* The first word was highly charged with emotion during the racial upheavals of the fifties and sixties. The second word is spooky today because of tensions in the job market and laws governing fair employment practices.

Prejudice is an attitude. *Discrimination* is an activity. *Prejudice* is the way we think. *Discrimination* is something we do.

A Closer Look at Prejudice

Prejudice is an opinion that results from very human conditions such as ignorance, fear, cultural inheritance, and a few random observations. It is usually irrational and nearly always incorrect or inaccurate. Prejudice causes us to think that all members of a group are the same; we don't look for or notice individual differences. We stereotype whole classes of people. "All men are alike." "Women are bad drivers." And you know what they say about Italians, Blacks, Arabs, Jews, Poles, Latinos, Republicans, Democrats, musicians, and preachers.

It is possible, of course, to notice things about groups of people that are true. There is no prejudice when you observe that women have more estrogen flowing in their systems than men do. It is not prejudice when you note that some groups have more skin pigmentation than others do. These statements are completely correct.

But try a little game. See how many undeniably correct statements you can make about any group of people that genuinely sets them apart from others. Think of things that absolutely include every member of that group. If you are honest with yourself you will be startled by how many of the imagined differences simply can't stand the test. You will see how insidious prejudice can be. To have prejudice is to *prejudge*.

Prejudicial stereotypes are difficult to overcome. So many people have believed them and passed them on through so many generations that they have taken on the appearance of fact. The entertainment industry, once amusing millions by proving the reality of stereotypes, has consciously attempted to break out of them. Portrayals of blacks as stupid, servile watermelon eaters who are afraid of ghosts has been replaced by images of highly competent blacks in positions of leadership and authority. Bloodthirsty Indians who had a limited vocabulary of grunts and sign language are increasingly pictured today as genuine human beings with intelligence, sensitivity, and a deep spirituality. On TV a woman works side by side with a man showing us how to remodel a house.

Prejudice, then, is a judgmental attitude that can endure for a lifetime. While it can be applied to anything from food to cars, in this book we are thinking specifically about how it affects our *relationships* with people. Prejudice prepares us to respond to another person in an unfavorable way because of that individual's group category. Prep-school students look down on public-high-school students. Public-high-school students look down on preppies. It doesn't matter who they are or what they are really like.

Once I was walking down Broad Street in Richmond, Virginia. As I crossed the driveway by the Sears store an irate motorist shook his fist at me and yelled, "You (bleep bleep) Virginia hick!" I still don't have any idea what I did to offend him. Since it is obvious that he was prejudiced, he probably saw what he expected to see.

A Closer Look at Discrimination

Discrimination is what happens when our prejudices control our behavior. It is an open demonstration of our attitude.

Discrimination places heavy psychological and spiritual burdens on its targets. He or she may begin to feel inferior and worthless. Self-criticism, even self-hatred, often results. In 1947 an experiment was conducted with black children from three to seven years of age. They were shown pairs of dolls, one dark brown, the other with light flesh tones. The children were asked which doll was nicer, which one they would like to play with, which doll was the prettiest. Two-thirds of the black children preferred the dolls with the lighter skin. They disliked the dolls that most resembled themselves. Similar results were obtained from other studies. The Supreme Court mentioned these findings in the ruling that outlawed segregation.

The same thing has been discovered in research on American women. A vast study in 1968 found that both sexes rated men as being more independent, objective, active, logical, leading, ambitious, and knowledgeable about the world than women. Women were seen as being more tactful, tender, and sensitive to the feelings of others. When these people (more than a thousand of them) were asked to rate the desirability of the various traits, three-quarters of them preferred the "male" qualities.

My wife and I have been building a little cottage in the woods for the past two years on our vacations and days off. To keep it affordable, we are doing everything ourselves with a little guidance and help from friends who are experienced in the various aspects of house building. One evening after a hard day's labor we went to a restaurant for dinner. I was into electrical wiring at that point and took a book into the restaurant to look up a few facts while we were waiting to be served. When we went to the counter to pay for the meal, Anna was holding the book. The woman clerk became very excited when she saw the title on the cover, *Modern Electrical Wiring*.

"You do wiring!" she said. "I once rewired a lamp! They told me I couldn't do it, but I did. They said it was a man's job. I did it, and I have never been so proud in my life!"

The dangerous fallout of discrimination is that it frequently convinces the recipients that it is justifiable. Stereotypical expectations become a self-fulfilling prophecy. If you believe you won't be able to succeed, you will stop trying. You become willing to fail. If I expect you to be lazy and irresponsible, you may well become lazy and irresponsible.

Researchers wanting to know whether or not the expectations of prejudice could cause teachers to discriminate in a way that would affect students' classroom performance set up an ingenious experiment. When school began in the fall, classes of elementary students were given a fake IQ test. The children's teachers were then informed that the test indicated that certain students would show a rapid intellectual spurt during the year. They were little geniuses in the bud.

The truth is, the "geniuses" were randomly selected. The names of about a fifth of each class were given to each teacher. What the researchers accomplished by this was to create positive expectations toward one group of students in each class. Four months after this seed was planted the randomly selected students began to show high scores, performing better than the others. By the end of the year they were far ahead of the others. First and second graders for whom these artificially high expectations were created were doing impressively better, and their outstanding performance carried over to the next year.

The teachers themselves gave the best grades and the highest personal ratings to the artificial group of "smarties" and the average and poorer grades to the others. The 80 percent of the children who did not get in the random sample were rated as being less curious, less interested, less happy, and less likely to succeed. In short, the teachers had created what they expected to find. Some students got ahead, not because they were actually more intelligent, but because their teachers expected them to do better.

The experiment, conducted by Rosenthal and Jacobson in 1968, was hotly disputed. But many similiar studies confirm that social expectations do influence behavior. The evidence is that targets of discrimination have a tendency to become what they are expected to be, whether better or worse. All people are not affected to the same degree, and much depends upon when and where the discrimination is taking place.

Discrimination is directed toward all kinds of groups. It may be on the basis of race, religion, national origin, age, sex, handicap, hairline, brand of sneakers, or just about anything. As we enter a new century, we are gradually seeing more and more successful challenges to discrimination in all its ugly forms.

In Christ There Is No East or West

Prejudice is dangerous. It can fan the flames of bitter hostilities among all kinds of God's children. While more and more overt discrimination is being made illegal in America, this does not totally eliminate the underlying prejudice. It simply helps a little by mixing people who may ordinarily avoid each other. Negative stereotypes are less common in the entertainment industry. Racist and sexist policies in public places are largely a thing of the past. Many parents are careful not to teach the old prejudices to their children. But prejudice remains a persistent part of human experience. New prejudices develop every day as people live together.

Bringing different kinds of people together is not enough in itself to overcome prejudice. Sometimes the closeness only results in increased antagonism. Four elements are crucial for reducing or eliminating prejudice.

- *There must be an equality of status,* and each group of people needs to perceive the equality as genuine. That famous line from Orwell's *Animal Farm,* "Some are more equal than others," is enough to destroy any hope for progress. Social contact will reduce prejudice only when genuine equality is present.

- *There must be common goals.* All groups involved need to feel they are working together to achieve something worthwhile.

- *There must be some clear success.* Prejudice will be reduced when some victory is won by working together. Close friendships among different kinds of people are common on championship athletic teams. Failure invites pointing to "the others" as scapegoats.

- *There must be participation in making decisions.* Prejudice is reduced when everyone has equal opportunity to express an opinion and control is not in the hands of a few.

To overcome personal prejudices we need to educate ourselves about the other groups of people. If we distrust people we don't know very well, then becoming more aware of them as individuals and as a culture will increase trust.

We saw in chapter 2 that Christianity represents something radically new in the world. "If anyone is in Christ, he is a new creation; the old has gone, the new has come!" (2 Corinthians 5:17). New attitudes replace old attitudes. New values, new standards, new relationships with others come into existence in Christ. The new life hits us hardest where prejudice thrives.

The minute we come to Christ and acknowledge we are God's child, when we are baptized into the household of God, our relationships undergo a change. God becomes our Father. Our old estrangement from God is gone. "To all who received him, to those who believed in his name, he gave the right to become children of God" (John 1:12).

This affects our relationship with God's other children. The two are inseparable. *If we love God, we will love each other.* If our love for others is restricted or narrowed by prejudice, then this is clear evidence that our love for God is not yet complete.

The New Testament gives us a very practical application of this.

> As believers in our glorious Lord Jesus Christ, don't show favoritism. Suppose a man comes into your meeting wearing a gold ring and fine clothes, and a poor man in shabby clothes also comes in. If you show special attention to the man wearing fine clothes and say, "Here's a good seat for you," but say to the poor man, "You stand there" or "Sit on the floor by my feet," have you not discriminated among yourselves and become judges with evil thoughts?"

If you really keep the royal law found in Scripture, "Love your neighbor as yourself," you are doing right. But if you show favoritism, you sin and are convicted by the law as lawbreakers. *James 2:1-4, 8-9*

Prejudice and snobbery are completely out of place in the new attitude of being Christian. They are replaced by a feeling of humility. If, by the grace of God, I have come to Christ, I am grateful for the privilege. I understand he offers this privilege to everyone. There can be no arrogance on my part.

Competition may be the driving force in sports, politics, and business, but cooperation is what produces our greatest achievements. From the building of a pyramid to the survival of a colonial village, cooperation is what makes it happen. We do what we do best for the good of the community. Others do their part. One is a farmer, another a carpenter, yet another a miller or a merchant. All are needed for the good of the group.

Cooperation is living at its best. Working together preserves and promotes life. I will never forget something I saw during a minor flood in Florida. Excessive rains had saturated the soil, and rivers were running out of their banks. An odd patch of material came floating by where I was standing. It was about the size of a platter and not more than an inch above the water. As it drew nearer I realized that it was a cluster of fire ants. As much as I detested and feared those painful little insects, I had to respect what I was seeing. Hundreds of them had locked limbs together, forming a floating island, sort of a Noah's ark, for the rest of the colony. Of course, the ones on the bottom had drowned long before they were swept by my feet. But even in death, they stuck together, preserving the life of the others. Competitiveness in this case would have been deadly. Costly cooperation brought survival.

Most communities have more than one church. People sort themselves out according to personal preferences. Ordinarily, the various denominations peacefully coexist. Sometimes they are openly antagonistic toward each other. In either case, those who prefer no church relationship at all are often frowned upon by those who do. I vividly recall what happened in one particular community when a famous hurricane devastated the area with floods. It no longer mattered whether you were Baptist or Methodist, pagan or Pentecostal. Because of the great loss of life and property, the survivors were needy human beings. Everyone pitched in. Neighbor helped neighbor. Churches from far away sent clothes and important supplies. Common suffering closed every gap between individuals and groups of people.

People have a natural tendency to cooperate. We will get together whenever we can. Joining groups and organizations is a very human behavior. This close contact with others ordinarily results in individual accommodation and compromise for the good of the group. It is relatively rare for association with others to produce fighting and injury. Most people want to cooperate within the structures of the group.

But it is folly to pit one group against another outside of recreational games. The world will be a safe and enjoyable place only when everyone overcomes ingrained prejudice and can agree that we all have one Creator, one Father.

6

IN HARMONY WITH NATURE

There is a signature of wisdom and power impressed on the works of God, which evidently distinguishes them from the feeble imitations of men—Not only the splendor of the sun, but the glimmering light of the glow worm, proclaims his glory.

John Newton

The belief that God created us and the world we live in is in no way threatened or compromised by the efforts of modern science to understand and explain it all. Some of the most awed and reverent people on earth are those who peer through telescopes and monitor screens at the depths of the universe. Surgeons admit they are sometimes moved by the beauty and intricacy of human organs. In every field of scientific exploration, the more we learn, the less we know. A Creator God remains an important and inescapable solution to a puzzle of vast proportions.

71

When we accept the fact that "The earth is the Lord's, and everything in it, the world, and all who live in it" (Psalm 24:1), it becomes imperative that we view ourselves in relationship with *all* of God's creation. Our reconciliation is not confined to God and other people; it extends to forests, lakes, rivers, creeks, seas, deserts, farms, gardens, lawns, rights-of-way, trash dumps, road beds, parking lots, mineral mines, the air we breathe, and every nook and corner of this planet. Future generations will have to come to terms with the fact that it also includes every scrap of material existing in the universe around us.

In Genesis, God instructs us this way:

> "Be fruitful and increase in number; fill the earth and subdue it. Rule over the fish of the sea and the birds of the air and over every living creature that moves on the ground." *Genesis 1:28*

Since the industrial revolution, most interpretations of that passage of Scripture have supported the belief that the natural resources of the earth are here for us to exploit as we wish. God gave us all this stuff for our profit and pleasure.

Our generation, awakened by the shock of death and destruction, is beginning to realize that ruling over the earth involves care and oversight. In the second chapter of Genesis we read, "The LORD God took the man and put him in the Garden of Eden *to work it and take care of it*" (verse 15, italics mine.)

The Problems Are Obvious

The earth is a finite place. There is a definite limit to its mineral deposits, fossil fuels, and component chemicals. Many mines and pits are already exhausted. The renewable nature of surface vegetation and wildlife is being ignored in the name of jobs and profits. Self-cleansing rivers will take generations to recover from the pollution of our time. The Bible's words are being proved true in this generation: "This world in its present form is passing away" (1 Corinthians 7:31).

Insects imported accidentally in commerce and intentionally by experimenters with a dream of riches are having a devastating effect upon our country's flora. Recall some of their names: Mexican bean beetle; Japanese beetle; gypsy moth; African "killer" bees.

Valuable stands of native chestnut trees have been lost to an imported blight. Elm trees succumb to an imported virus. Even the rats in our city sewers came to our ports on ships.

Ecology is no longer the private study of a few oddball specialists in the upper hallways of college classroom buildings. It has become a major concern of thoughtful people everywhere. It is on the mind of a Chesapeake waterman who wonders where all the oysters have gone. It is on the mind of a child listening to his grandfather tell of the time he shot a hundred squirrels in one day. It is on the mind of the homeowner whose faucets discharge undrinkable water. It is on the mind of an ivory carver who keeps an elephant tusk in a safe. It is on the mind of a potato farmer watching the Colorado beetles stripping the leaves from his plants in spite of the powerful and expensive insecticides he has sprayed on them.

Behind the pitiful observations and the wondering that goes with them are two points well worth pondering: What if we louse it up for ourselves? What if we use our children's portion?

None of us have ever seen a living passenger pigeon. I have looked at a stuffed one in Washington's Natural History Museum. Another generation killed them all. They didn't think it was possible. They were so numerous in Midwestern skies in the nineteenth century that great flocks of them could hide the sun. Migrating waves of them would take all day to pass. Shooting a passenger pigeon was like cutting a blade of grass on a football field with a pair of scissors. It made no perceptible difference. It became fashionable to put pigeon feathers in hats. Using them for target practice became great sport. We still have the term "stool pigeon" in our vocabulary from the time when a live, fluttering passenger pigeon on a wooden stool decoyed others to their destruction. People who enjoyed killing passenger pigeons were perplexed when their numbers began to diminish, but they were sure that great droves would return next year. Not all that long ago a boy with a BB gun shot the last wild passenger pigeon ever seen. The one the taxidermist fixed for the museum was a captive bird, the last of her species. Hunters had to begin shooting clay pigeons.

I have no doubt at all that if it were possible for people to shoot out the stars with rifles, there would be no stars in our sky tonight.

> The earth is broken up,
> > the earth is split asunder,

the earth is thoroughly shaken.
The earth reels like a drunkard,
    it sways like a hut in the wind;
so heavy upon it is the guilt of its rebellion
    that it falls—never to rise again. *Isaiah 24:19-20*

Ecological Reconciliation

The Bible assures us, over and over again, that human life will be better, more prosperous and more enjoyable, when we take care of the natural resources God has given us in a responsible manner. God's law recorded in Leviticus says,

> "If you follow my decrees and are careful to obey my commands, I will send you rain in its season, and the ground will yield its crops and the trees of the field their fruit. Your threshing will continue until grape harvest and the grape harvest will continue until planting, and you will eat all the food you want and live in safety in your land." *Leviticus 26:3-5*

The music of the Psalms sings the idea.

> May the peoples praise you, O God;
>   may all the peoples praise you.
> Then the land will yield its harvest,
>   and God, our God, will bless us. *Psalm 67:5-6*

People living in an urban society (and this, by far, includes most of us) easily lose contact with the earth. A few may notice and appreciate a brave dandelion growing in the crack of a sidewalk, but the beautiful cycle of seedtime and harvest is out of sight and beyond awareness. Eggs don't come from clucking chicken hens; they come from refrigerators. Grapes are not the heady fragrance of the end of summer; they are available all year in the supermarket. Watermelon is as handy in January as it is in July. Fresh fruits and vegetables in tremendous variety are on the shelf for the picking at just about any time. With processing, all kinds of food can be preserved and sold without fear of spoilage. Meal worms, rancid flour, and stale cereal are things of the past.

Consider the respect of a farmer or rancher for the ways of nature. An arsenal of herbicides and insecticides are available, of course. There is also a tremendous armory of machinery to work and water the soil. But most of the farmers I know are people who still take a searching look at the sky every day. They feel a special stimulation when the first warm southern breeze stirs in late winter. The sun rises earlier and sets later. Freshly turned earth has a living fragrance, a promising odor that invites seeding. With joy and satisfaction, the job is done. The fields are a sight of perfection. Everything is smooth, unblemished by stray weeds or sickly plants.

Soon enough, tender shoots are breaking the surface of the soil, reaching for the sun. Soon enough, something arrives to eat them. Soon enough, unintentional plants emerge to compete. The struggle is on. Rain becomes a precious commodity.

Eventually there will be open blossoms and foraging bees, followed by seeds now multiplied hundreds of times—corn, beans, wheat, barley, oats. The day will come when there will be great piles of squash, tomatoes, and potatoes. The air will grow cool again, the days, shorter. It will be the season for turnips, pumpkins, and kale.

Meat will be butchered and put away, firewood gathered, barn doors closed. The farmer can sing with the psalmist, "Then the land will yield its harvest, and God, our God, will bless us" (Psalm 67:6). The snows will come. The farmer will rest a little and wait for spring.

Imagine the respect for God's creation by a member of a hunting-gathering community in modern or ancient times:

Dawn gently nudges you awake. On a nearby shrub dew glistens like jewels on a spider web. Standing, you feel the forest floor beneath your feet and between your toes. Breathing deeply of fresh, clean air, you are grateful for another day.

All around you is life—life that sustains life. You understand, even as your stomach rumbles, that everything alive must eat in order to remain alive. Life consumes life, but life goes on. The plant feeds on the earth. A beetle feeds on the plant. A toad feeds on the beetle. A snake feeds on the toad. A hawk feeds on the snake. The earth feeds on the hawk. But plants, beetles, toads, snakes, and hawks continue.

The world you inhabit is a treasure store of the things you and your community need to survive. It produces far more than enough for everyone. But you take only what you need, and then only at the proper moment. You have a deep respect for nests, females, and young. Ownership is not your primary concern. Everything that exists belongs to everything else that exists. There is a harmony of relationship so clear you can almost hear it. You will not foul a pool of water, because you and other creatures will drink from it. Gratitude and respect are part of your daily existence.

Most of us are not farmers or ranchers. It is not likely that anyone reading this book is a hunter-gatherer. Consequently, we have a huge difficulty to overcome. Our awareness of the greater world and universe can be severely restricted by the limitations of our experience. Our world of apartment and office is a tiny one. Life on this limited scale may satisfy you, but it cannot be sustained indefinitely without responsible people paying attention to the care of the whole earth. Death is but a breakdown of the agricultural transportation system away. If the trucks can't roll regularly to the loading docks with essential supplies, chaos is only hours from your world.

Two unhappy facts about ourselves are forever threatening to disturb our security. The first is the fact that people are nasty. Not all of us, but enough to matter. Ask anyone who cleans public restrooms for a living. Talk with the people who collect roadside litter. Look around a stadium after a ball game. Recall the scenes of mud and debris following Woodstock. An explorer in our time says he discovers rusting junk cars on isolated mountain peaks. Jacques Cousteau reports the oceans are dying in a floating avalanche of plastic. We are one of the few species that foul our own nest.

The other fact is that people are greedy. Not all of us, but enough to matter. Profit is a blinding motivator. If the things of the earth can be turned into money, then let us turn them into money, and let us do it in the most efficient way! Let someone get in the way, protesting the unnecessary and unwise wholesale destruction of, say, a Brazilian rainforest, and he will be ruthlessly gunned down. Our world is a place where a few can sell the inheritance of us all for a bowl of instant financial porridge.

One of Christ's great works is to change these ugly tendencies in people. If the perpetrators themselves cannot be changed, they can at least be controlled by a world grown weary of irresponsible living. Much of the damage can be repaired. In time, even lifeless rivers will purge themselves. Health is recoverable. Intelligent use is all that is required. Concern about these things is becoming a great part of the younger generation's consciousness. In increasing numbers, people are wanting to make a difference.

John Thompson was a member of Quaker Memorial Presbyterian Church in Lynchburg, Virginia. In his retirement he began to take an interest in the considerable acreage of church property that surrounds the building. It is a large, triangular-shaped city block containing a Quaker meeting house built in 1792, an ancient cemetery enclosed behind a stone wall, a parking lot, and grass enough to intimidate the most ardent mower.

John decided a few flower beds would be nice. He planted some marigolds and impatiens against the foundation of the church. He worked and mulched a large bed of azaleas already existing behind the chancel. Over a period of years he expanded his flower beds to every lovely corner of the property, tending them almost daily in the summer. Where common grass would not grow in the shade, he planted a shade-loving grass. Others, catching his spirit, helped him set out trees of many kinds to eventually replace the grand old oaks that were nearing maturity.

Eventually cars zooming by on the street began to slow down. People took pictures. When John died, a television crew came to do a story. John Thompson left the world more beautiful than he found it. In your own way, in your own place, you can, too.

Things You Can Do

The bumper sticker says, "Think Globally. Act Locally." As Nehemiah understood, the way to repair a broken wall is to have people work on the section nearest their home. Even within the limits of a small daily orbit, there are some practical and helpful things you can do to achieve ecological reconciliation. A few ideas are listed below. Not all of them will be for you, and you will certainly be able to think of others.

- *Open your eyes to the life around you.* There are living things that could use your attention all around your neighborhood.

- *Do you see any birds?* Few places of the world are without birds. Even in a congested downtown environment you will likely find English sparrows, starlings, and pigeons. If you live in the suburbs, there are songbirds all around you. A window feeder in winter will attract birds you may have never seen before. I still remember my excitement upon seeing my first purple finch. I didn't know such a bird existed! They are all but invisible to the eye until they come to feed. There will be dozens of other birds you have missed. Just wait until you watch a tiny chickadee hold a sunflower seed in its feet and pound away with its bill until it can get at the nourishment inside. Feed the birds—especially in winter.

- *Do you want to get even more involved?* Many who begin by feeding birds are drawn quite naturally into bird clubs. Perhaps you can participate in a bird count. Maybe you can identify bird habitats and spot any threats encroaching upon them.

- *Support efforts to protect aquatic life.* Buy brands of tuna that are caught by fisherman who watch out for dolphins. Return a fish to the water after you have enjoyed catching it.

- *Conserve water all year round.* Turn off the spigot every moment you can. Water your lawn and garden at night, and then only when it is absolutely necessary.

- *Go ahead and watch one of those nature shows on TV.* You may find life in a beehive almost as engaging as a soap opera.

- *Take your family to a wildlife rehabilitation or education center.* Spend some time helping children discover the wonders of nature.

- *Get out of bed one morning before sunrise.* Be still and silent. Watch and listen as the world around you wakes up.

- *Find a place out in the country where there are no lights to blot out the stars.* With a guidebook or star chart, try to find a few of the easy constellations. If you have binoculars, take a closer look at the Pleiades, Orion's sword, the double star in the handle of the big dipper, and the craters of the moon. Let your mind wander around out there in the vastness of God's creation.

- *Reflect on the earth as a display of the glory of God the way the Bible does.*

In the year that King Uzziah died, I saw the Lord seated on a throne, high and exalted, and the train of his robe filled the temple. Above him were seraphs, each with six wings: With two wings they covered their faces, with two they covered their feet, and with two they were flying. And they were calling to one another:

"Holy, holy, holy is the LORD Almighty;
the whole earth is full of his glory." *Isaiah 6:1-3*

The glory of the Lord fills the whole earth. *Numbers 14:21*

- *Check around your house for dangerous chemicals.* Take a look under your sink. Anything there that could harm an inquisitive child? Go through your garage, basement, or tool shed. Explore ways to dispose of toxic wastes.

- *Support environmental legislation if it is reasonable.* The nature of law-making sometimes produces legislation that is idiotic. Decide for yourself. If it makes sense, write your representative an encouraging letter.

- *Purchase a fuel-efficient car.* Keep it tuned. Alter your driving style. Walk when you have only a short trip. Use public transportation.

- *Hunt with a camera.* If you use a gun or rifle, use it responsibly. Kill only what you intend to eat. Kill, if you must, to control (but not eradicate) an animal population.

- *Compost waste vegetable matter, including leaves in the autumn.* The results will work magic in your garden, and you will help save landfill space. Plant ground covers to reduce the amount of mowing around your home. Think about it a long time before you spread fertilizers and chemicals. Is a little clover in your grass all that bad? Is there any way you can think of a yellow dandelion flower as beautiful?

- *Make a thorough energy audit of your home.* Do you have enough insulation? Is your heating and air conditioning efficient? Can you switch to some high-tech light bulbs that save electricity? Adjust all the thermostats you can find. The one on the wall is just the beginning. There's also one in the refrigerator, in the freezer, on the hot water heater, and elsewhere. You will save money while saving energy.

- *Are you a woodworking hobbyist?* Don't buy rare woods from tropical forests or anywhere else unless you can be certain sustainable forestry techniques were used in harvesting it.

- *Look for a place to plant some trees.*

- *Patronize a farmer's market.* Spend an extra dollar for something organically grown.

- *Meditate on these verses of Scripture:*

  For God was pleased to have all his fullness dwell in him, and through him to reconcile to himself all things, whether things on earth or things in heaven, by making peace through his blood, shed on the cross. Once you were alienated from God and were enemies in your minds because of your evil behavior. But now he has reconciled you by Christ's physical body through death to present you holy in his sight, without blemish and free from accusation. *Colossians 1:19-22*

• *Pray this prayer from Nehemiah:*

You alone are the LORD. You made the heavens, even the highest heavens, and all their starry host, the earth and all that is on it, the seas and all that is in them. You give life to everything, and the multitudes of heaven worship you. *Nehemiah 9:6*

7

GETTING ALONG AT WORK

Labor is prior to, and independent of, capital. Capital is only the fruit of labor, and could never have existed if labor had not first existed. Labor is the superior of capital, and deserves much the higher consideration.
Abraham Lincoln, First Annual Message to Congress, December 3, 1861

An alarming number of Americans do not enjoy their work. Many are glad to have a job, a source of income, but derive no personal satisfaction from what they are doing or the way in which they doing it. A recent study by Northwestern National Life Insurance Company discovered that 46 percent of us are concerned about our job. We are working under killing pressure, trying to prove our worth, striving to meet deadlines, and attempting to keep elusive profits up.

The fun has gone out of Monday morning. The work place has become something of a nuclear reactor chamber. The heat is on and the pressure is up. The pot is boiling.

Modern Maladies

Mergers are commonplace in today's business environment. Viewed from the top, a merger is a way to save taxes and increase net worth. As experienced by the work force, however, a merger is a threat to job security, a boon for real estate sales, and it leads to obsolescence of previously acquired skills. In many cases, a merger means one person will do the work of two or three. There is suddenly too much to do and not enough time to do it.

Computers allow incredible record keeping and control. Provided the data is entered correctly, they can access tons of detailed information in a flash. It is impossible to conduct business today without computers. They are supposed to be great laborsaving devices. If the software developers were to stop working, that could possibly become true someday. As it is, the revisions and changes faced by hundreds of thousands of workers sitting at a computer eat up hour upon unproductive hour. Training sessions and fifteen-pound ring binders become the masters of our time. Meanwhile the internal clock is ticking; the deadline for a particular mainframe activity is 2:00 P.M. Is there anything significant in that ominous name, *terminal?*

Stress at work leads to all kinds of problems for us. Fifty years ago ulcers were the popular fringe benefit. "Ulcers?" asked the classic boss. "I don't get 'em. I *give* 'em!" Our medical experts indicate that today ulcers are not anywhere near the top of the list. They've been beaten out by depression, exhaustion, heart disease, hypertension, insomnia, colitis, and various aches from head to foot. Job stress is also a major contributor to alcoholism and divorce.

We've become an edgy population. Everyone is answerable to someone above them. The one at the top has the stockholders to please. Performance reviews are a game of words that often enough miss reality. Praise a worker and she will expect a raise. Be objectively cool and he will be demoralized. So much is at risk.

Is it any wonder that in the atmosphere of the average modern American place of work people sometimes have difficulty getting along? There have always been rivalries, of course. Everyone in a higher position has someone gunning for the spot, wanting the job and its salary for themselves. Those who share the closed environment of an office, store, or plant engage in the same struggles and conflicts people experience elsewhere in their lives. The problem is that when it happens at work it becomes a threat to basic security. You can quit participating in choir practice and skip the bridge game, but by going to work you pay your bills and save for the future. The stakes are highest there. It is vital that we find ways to reduce stress by getting along with others at work.

Survival Skills

Endless fighting is a tragic waste. There comes a time to call a truce and get on with life. Sometimes a cease fire can be accomplished with surprising ease by nothing more than direct confrontation. I did this once with remarkable simplicity. I was a college freshman at a school where a little hazing was still practiced by the sophomores. Something about me attracted the attention of a particular sophomore, who went out of his way to harass me. After a few weeks of this nonsense I walked over to him while he was eating dinner with his friends and said, "If you are trying to make my life here miserable, you are succeeding." He looked at me with a wide-eyed astonishment that surprised me. There were no words that I can remember, but his startled expression seemed to say, "I didn't realize that! Please excuse me. I'm sorry." Maybe I didn't understand the full dynamics of the situation and was totally out of order, but I can report that he never bothered me again. You figure it out.

There are better methods that result in genuine reconciliation. All I did was get rid of a pest. I did not make a friend. Our relationship was only tangential. We did not have to work together in anything at all. We merely occupied some of the same space at the same time. If something important had depended upon our cooperation as members of a team, my solution to the problem would have been ill-advised.

Suppose someone you work with every day is an "adult child." Our work places are full of people who use infantile behavior in an effort to get through another day. They pout. They scream. They puff and groan when things do not go their way. They tattle and have a huge need for the approval of their superiors. They are territorial and possessive. They wear their feelings on their sleeve and almost seem eager to be offended. They may do their job well, sometimes carrying more than their share of the load, but they are pure grief to anyone working nearby. Conflict is inevitable. What can you do?

- *Begin your approach with something easy to fix.* Take the path of least resistance. Some bones of contention are more important than others. Dig up the simplest as casually as possible. A good salesman understands that the smallest concession is a very big foot in the door. Try to work out an agreement together on an emotionless detail. This may interrupt a cycle of behavior that would prevent additional change.

- *Say something nice.* Instead of talking yourself into a destructive corner the way heads of state sometimes talk themselves into war, make a conscious attempt to speak constructively. Look closely for something positive in the other person and reinforce it. If it is honest and sincere, it will go a long way toward improving your relations with each other.

- *Be fair.* Try to take yourself out of it and be as objective as possible. Don't let the highly charged issue of competence get into your discussion. Rational adult discussion avoids some thorny places.

- *Do your best to help the other person feel important.* Avoid put-downs as though they were snakes. Put the spotlight on what is right rather than what is wrong. Praises are better than condemnations. A supportive approach will always be the most productive.

Family Businesses

When a company is owned and operated by people related to each other, smooth cooperation meets some unique difficulties. There are some sensitivities in this situation that are not much of a problem in a large corporate setting. Because there are many family businesses in every community, the subject merits special attention here.

Anyone having some education and/or business sense is capable of solving typical business problems. Any good business mind can find ways to minimize taxes. The competition can be taken on. Unions respond to negotiation. Even governmental regulations can be tolerated. But dealing with relatives who own a part of the business is tricky and full of hazards. Business school will take you only so far.

Suppose your children threaten to move the grandchildren out of town if they don't get their way. It has been known to happen. What do you do? How do you work with family members who seem to be constantly at each other's throats? If your business partner is your spouse, how do you manage a disagreement?

Most families want to continue living together in spite of their contests of will and judgment. The natural bond of love and blood is stronger than the firmest business opinions. Heavy-handed unilateral action is out of place in this context. And yet, power plays between spouses, parents, children, in-laws, and other relatives tend to fester like untreated open wounds. Time only makes things worse. Eventually these problems may threaten the business itself.

One way to repair such situations is to introduce an outside influence. An objective view removed from any emotional involvement can work wonders. This does not necessarily mean you should hire a consultant. That could be helpful, but in most cases it is unnecessary. The person to referee the fairness of a discussion does not have to be from outside the business. The important thing is that he or she is outside the conflict.

Consider adding some "outsiders" to your board of directors. This dilution can be as healthy as pouring fresh water in an old aquarium. You may be surprised by the quickness with which a new board member can see the root cause of a problem. I see this happen regularly when a church board rotates a third of its membership every year. New faces bring new ideas. Old snags and taboos tend to weaken.

There are likely more than two sides to any issue. No one will be absolutely and completely correct. People who are close to each other have a tendency to speak less guardedly when they have a strong opinion about something. Family members can be brutal with their criticism of each other. It is out of order, but we do it anyway. It may become necessary to bring in someone from the outside. This will necessitate exposing everyone to possibly severe review. If your business's best interests are in danger, invasion of privacy and personal risk may be a small price to pay. Competent advisors have diplomatic ways of pointing out our greed, overconfidence, presumption, and selfishness.

Above all, people working together in a family business need to understand clearly that the only battle worth winning is the one with the competition. Internal conflict wastes valuable time and energy. It inhibits progress, productivity, and profits. Energy blown away on a family feud, no matter how righteous the cause, is energy drained down a very hungry black hole.

Four Keys to Reconciliation

As I prepared to write this book, I read through a large collection of professional literature on conflict management.

After a while I could see that most of these books and papers are saying the same thing. Each researcher approaches the question from a unique angle, but the results are consistent. Four important means toward reconciliation at work (and elsewhere) rise to the top of every discussion.

Collaboration

Consider this first. Collaboration is by far the best way to resolve conflict. If the contest is a two-way split, both parties will be satisfied. If the problem has grown to involve several camps of opinion with numerous people on every side, collaboration will bring a resolution that will be pleasing to more of them than will any other approach. Because everyone owns a part of the action, there is an excellent probability that the resolution will be effective and remain so.

Collaboration brings people together. They co-labor to find a solution. Any decision is a group decision. A clear opportunity to participate on an equal basis with everyone else gives every person a sense of gaining, not losing, power. It also provides the best possible way to hear the other sides of the issue.

This process takes time and effort. Because it requires real involvement on the part of those who are in disagreement, collaboration is more difficult than other paths toward reconciliation. It can sometimes be painful or risky. A few individuals will feel threatened at first. Some may even object to attempting to solve a problem this way because they are reluctant to become involved in such depth.

Collaboration can work only when people believe a mutually agreeable resolution is possible. As hopeless as any situation may seem, the problem probably has an answer. It will take searching, and it may be a struggle. But if everyone will agree to go through the bother of searching for it, good things can happen.

There is nothing mystical about the collaboration process. There are no tricks known only to a few specialists. It takes nothing more than common sense. An understanding of the principles of Christianity will go a long way toward ensuring success. The problem is that when people are fighting they become excited and irrational. At such times it is easy to set aside common sense and forget what Christ has taught us.

How do you get started? Someone has to take the first step. Why not let it be you?

- *Go ahead and take the risk of opening the conversation in a friendly manner.* Early in the process, make it clear that you are willing to cooperate. By now you will admit to yourself that you may not have a monopoly on what is good and right. Let it be clear that you are willing to make concessions. Bring everyone involved into the discussion.

- *Consider sitting down and talking it over together in some unfamiliar location.* Neutral turf has great value in moments like these. If one place is associated with strife, another may convey the promise of peace. By all means get out of public view. Spectators, especially spectators who have taken sides, only confound the issue. You will be tempted to play to the audience rather than focus on what you are about. Getting in the damaging last word becomes very important when there's someone cheering you on. Instead of putting out the fire you will fan the flames if your supporters are watching and keeping score.

- *Remember that everyone participating wants to come out "smelling like a rose."* No one will participate who wants to appear to be anything other than an effective winner. The more heated the discussion, the more likely a person will take a do-or-die stand in order to save face. We all have our pride. Respect this. Collaborate as equals. If there is a real chance that we can engage in this process without losing our dignity, we will be less reluctant to participate.

- *Try to trust each other.* This will be difficult. Until the treachery is discovered, whoever is stabbing you in the back will smile and greet you warmly. Once the underhanded business is out in the open, trust will evaporate like dew on an August morning. Avoidance is ordinarily the next behavior. You can help restore trust by demonstrating that you will not respond in an antagonistic manner. Give the other persons reason to believe that you would honestly welcome an opportunity to compromise. Force yourself to give the others involved the benefit of the doubt. Whatever has already happened, try to trust them, too. A forgiving spirit will go a long way on this one.

- *Look for patterns.* Most conflict is a repetition of a game already played many times. Back off a bit and think it through. Is there a cycle that everyone needs to work to break?

- *Talk it over in a caring, open, nondefensive way.* Be absolutely certain that everyone has an equal opportunity to express ideas and concerns. Restrain the impulse to respond judgmentally to anything others say. A groan, a sigh, a raised eyebrow is all it takes to destroy someone's participation. There is no way everyone will agree with what a person says. You would not be collaborating this way if you already had a consensus of opinion. Encourage everyone to keep calm and wait for a turn.

Negotiation

When applied to the right problem, negotiation can be a simple process that brings with it a high success ratio. Many issues, of course, are not negotiable. If the difficulty is a concept, an attitude, or an ethical or moral judgment, negotiation is the wrong tool to apply. On the other hand, if it is a question of behavior, it may be the best.

Negotiation works when each participant in a disagreement has something that can be given up in trade. One surrenders this; another surrenders that. It works like old-fashioned bartering. I will give you a basket of eggs in exchange for a ball of yarn. No one gets everything, but everyone gets something.

This method is placed in second position because the results are not nearly as satisfying to the participants as collaboration. The sense of ownership is not as complete. Even when people negotiate cooperatively they feel a little coerced. Trust levels are not very high. The United States and the former Soviet Union negotiated nuclear arms reductions, but it will take continued inspections to make sure the parties are faithful to the agreement.

When negotiating it is important to look for options no one has thought about. Sometimes we think our only alternatives are A and B. Think some more. Is there a C? Could there possibly be a D? The more possibilities you place on the table the better. The answer could be as simple as taking turns.

If you agree to negotiation you must, by definition, be flexible. For it to work, you must be willing to yield a little here, a lot there. If you are rigid, if you are convinced you have the only position worth taking, then you are misleading yourself and others if you try to negotiate a settlement. Be clear about your own needs. Be realistic about the needs of others. When tradeoffs are made, see to it that they are of similar value. Buying a ten-carat diamond for a dollar is *not* a deal!

Communication

How many times have you heard it? "What we need around here is better communication." In most places of work, communication comes down to company newsletters or a memo posted on the bulletin board. Many businesses think they have really started communicating if they have a suggestion box. We are thinking here about something else entirely.

Communication is a two-way street. If one party has a transmitter and the other a receiver, some kind of message can be transferred. But they can't communicate. Communication involves both talking and listening. When you are not expressing what is really on your mind, your communication needs improvement. Communication has broken down when you are not perceiving the deepest desires and feelings of others.

If you sincerely want to communicate with others, start with yourself. Imagine you are watching yourself from the other side of the table. What do you see? Do you appear to be too delicate to survive the process? Are you easily hurt? If things don't go your way, is it already evident you will be crushed? Maybe you look fiercely angry. Is it clear you are ready to fight? Are you sending unspoken signals that you are an authority who is prepared to do some pressuring and arm-twisting? Then try something else. Attempt to imagine that you are the other person. Do the words you are hearing make any sense if you try to speak them? Can you understand why they are being said? Is anything implied that is not being directly uttered? When you begin to listen with as much energy as you use while speaking, you will begin to communicate.

Substance is the critical element in communication. People may be talking plainly and listening intently without accomplishing anything. Make sure that what you say is relevant to the issue at hand, and not merely speechmaking that makes you appear intelligent. If what is being said is inaccurate or misleading, communication becomes a negative process. Rumors and anonymous quotations should be ruled out by all participants.

Some have learned to use words as a defensive or offensive weapon. They can sweet-talk their way out of anything. They can browbeat an opponent into submission. If the attempt at communication becomes bogged down in meaningless jaw-boning, take a break. Go get a cup of coffee. If nothing new is being said after everyone has had a chance to refresh themselves, the time has come to try another way.

Placing spoken comments on paper helps. Let people express their own ideas on large sheets of paper with felt-tip pens. Let someone stand at a chalkboard or a blank flip chart and record what is being said. This will cut down on wasteful repetition. It also serves as concrete evidence that a person has been heard.

There is one great trap we must avoid: secondhand communication. Some people prefer to speak through another mouth. They work behind the scenes in secret. The telephone is their favorite communication tool. They send someone to a meeting armed with all kinds of half-truths and innuendoes. The result is that their expressions of dissatisfaction are translated through another personality. This is irresponsibility in more than one form. First of all, the listeners only hear the words that have been relayed. There is no eye contact, no tone of voice, facial expression, or body language to aid them in understanding what the person really feels. Secondly, there's no way for the absent person to get feedback. Since he (or she) is not *present,* his (or her) views are not subject to revision in light of new information or the insights of the group. Words thrown at us secondhand are like a rock hurled through the window with a message taped to it. How can we respond? Reconciliation is impossible.

When attempting to communicate, set it down as a rule that you will listen only to people who are actually present and participating. When peace is at stake, there is little value in absentee ballots or voting by proxy. Let everyone be willing to say, "I believe," rather than, "They say."

Executive Decision

This is a last resort because with an executive decision, someone is likely to be hurt. When every attempt at collaboration, negotiation, and communication fails, there is little remaining except for an authority to call the shot. In the same way that a schoolteacher sometimes must seat pupils on opposite sides of the classroom, workers may need to be separated. Was it a ball or a strike? The umpire himself may not know for sure. But he will have to call it one way or the other in order for the game to continue. Work-place conflicts that will not yield to collaboration, negotiation, or communication may require an authority who can make a final judgment.

Perhaps a truce can be held until an old-timer retires. Maybe someone is simply incompatible with the rest of the staff. It could be that an individual is being unfairly singled out for punishment. A good executive will attempt to learn the facts and then do what is best for the company.

I was once involved in a denominational process of closing a small, rural church. It was an unhappy, messy business. People still loved their church. The cemetery was well cared for. They did not want to attend the other church nearby. The process of reaching a decision took months of public and private discussion, and the decision of the denomination was ultimately defeated by the civil court. I would have preferred to have been somewhere else, doing another job.

Sometime later I was talking with a bishop in a hierarchical denomination. I asked him how he handled problems like that. He said, "I just close them!"

Getting On with the Job

The Lebow Company, a national training and consulting firm that specializes in team building, has come up with eight principles for running a healthy business.

1. Treat others with uncompromising truth.

2. Lavish trust on your associates.

3. Mentor unselfishly—be a teacher and a coach.

4. Be receptive to new ideas, regardless of their origin.

5. Take personal risks for the organization's sake.

6. Give credit where credit is due.

7. Do not touch dishonest dollars.

8. Put the interest of others before your own.

© The Lebow Company 1992. The Heroic Environment® is a registered trademark of the Lebow Company and is used by permission.

I can see nothing in this valuable list of winning ideas that is not a direct application of basic Christianity. There is not an original thought in them. What *is* new is their emphasis in a time when an opposing set of business dictums is far more popular. It is refreshing to see some guidelines for making money that recognize the worth of individual employees and promote participation by everyone. Perhaps there is hope for us after all.

8

COPING WITH CITY HALL

Society in every state is a blessing, but government, even in its best state, is but a necessary evil; in its worst state an intolerable one.
Thomas Paine, American revolutionary agitator and writer, *Common Sense*

The Associated Press recently carried a brief story that is an indicator of the times we live in. Block parties have been a tradition in many neighborhoods for years. They are a friendly way to keep in touch and to generate a sense of community that is so rare in most places. The neighbors gather once a year on someone's deck or yard, have a cookout, tell funny stories, and generally get acquainted.

"I thought the city had lost its mind," was the comment of the organizer when he returned from city hall after seeking permission to hold another party. The permit was going to cost him seventy-seven dollars—if he could get it at all. He had been instructed to collect the signatures of all the neighbors near the party and submit an application for the permit at least thirty days in advance.

"It was like jumping through all these hoops," the resident said.

The city had its points. It would cost twenty-seven dollars for a policeman to visit the neighborhood and verify all those signatures. The processing fee on the application was a flat fifty dollars. The process of approval would go through eight departments, including police, fire, public works, garbage collection, traffic engineering, and, of course, the city manager's office. The administrative assistant involved said, "I just don't understand why he's making it such a big deal. I don't think it is [expensive] when what you're being given is a private little area to have your party."

The block-party organizers, lulled by years of simpler times, were exasperated by the cumbersome bureaucracy. "They make it sound like we're trying to block off [a major thoroughfare] or an interstate." One of the party sponsors, resigned to the facts of life, concluded, "We should have known better. There's a tax on everything."

The Importance of Law

Life together has simply got to be regulated. Anarchy produces miserable living conditions. You may be slowed by traffic lights, but at some intersections you may not move again in your lifetime without them. Your neighbor may want to store dynamite in his garage, but the neighborhood will be safer if that is forbidden. Laws not only keep me in line and protect me from the schemes of thieves and robbers, they also simplify my life by giving me a steady, dependable under-girding. I can ordinarily count on how other people can be expected to behave. If I can safely assume that most people will not drive on the wrong side of the road, my daily existence is made a lot easier. The stress of living closely with other people is reduced. We will all get along better together if we can agree on some rules.

City hall, then, brings welcome order to our lives. We can settle the most serious disputes without resorting to violence or arbitrary judgments. The game is more enjoyable and play-able when we can agree on some rules, even when the regulations are sometimes a bother.

One day some people came to Jesus with a tricky question. "Is it right to pay taxes to Caesar or not? Should we pay or shouldn't we?" (Mark 12:14-15). It was one of those emotionally loaded questions that could sting our Lord whichever way he answered. If his reply was negative, then he would be in trouble with the Roman government. If he said yes, then he would lose popular support.

> But Jesus knew their hypocrisy. "Why are you trying to trap me?" he asked. "Bring me a denarius and let me look at it." They brought the coin, and he asked them, "Whose portrait is this? And whose inscription?"
> "Caesar's," they replied.
> Then Jesus said to them, "Give to Caesar what is Caesar's and to God what is God's." *Mark 12:15-17*

In this answer Jesus did far more than merely escape between the horns of a dilemma. He gave us an idea of tremendous value. He affirms the validity of governmental authority but gives ultimate obedience to God alone. This is the beginning of the doctrine that is so much in the news today—the separation of church and state.

The apostle Paul encouraged Christians to support the government.

> Everyone must submit himself to the governing authorities, for there is no authority except that which God has established. The authorities that exist have been established by God. Consequently, he who rebels against the authority is rebelling against what God has instituted, and those who do so will bring judgment on themselves. For rulers hold no terror for those who do right, but for those who do wrong. Do you want to be free from fear of the one in authority? Then do what is right and he will commend you. For he is God's servant to do you good. But if you do wrong, be afraid, for he does not bear the sword for nothing. He is God's servant, an agent of wrath to bring punishment on the wrongdoer. Therefore, it is necessary to submit to the authorities, not only because of possible punishment but also because of conscience.
>
> This is also why you pay taxes, for the authorities are God's servants, who give their full time to governing. Give everyone what you owe him: If you owe taxes, pay taxes; if revenue, then revenue; if respect, then respect; if honor, then honor. *Romans 13:1-7*

The New Testament is consistent in its instructions to Christians.

> Submit yourselves for the Lord's sake to every authority instituted among men: whether to the king, as the supreme

authority, or to governors, who are sent by him to punish those who do wrong and to commend those who do right. . . . Live as free men, but do not use your freedom as a cover-up for evil; live as servants of God. Show proper respect to everyone: Love the brotherhood of believers, fear God, honor the king. *1 Peter 2:13-14, 16-17*

The Problem with Law

The Christian church today has moved beyond the simple thinking of Christians in the first century or medieval times. "The divine right of kings" is not a widely accepted notion; there is simply too much recorded history to be reckoned with. As we enter the twenty-first century, the state is no longer simply accepted by Christians as something God-given even if it is imperfect. It is something human. Like everything human, it is open to criticism by rational judgment and moral conscience. If there is something wrong with it, it should be fixed. If it can't be fixed, let it be replaced. Supposedly, this is the purpose of free elections.

The problem is that laws are not always impartial. They may have been shaped by powerful lobby organizations. Some laws favor the rich and powerful while binding the poor and weak. Even when the law itself is impartial, it may not be administered that way by policemen and judges. Today's Christian will honor and obey the law without granting it a sanctity it does not possess. We can be grateful for its benefits without expecting it to be perfect. Nothing human is perfect. Government has an important purpose, and it needs the power to fulfill that purpose. But sometimes it falls under the care of people who distort its purpose and use its power for their own selfish reasons. Human rights are among the most precious achievements of the last five centuries of political history. But these rights are still far from secure. Christians are always on guard, ready to face down any state or group that threatens those rights. "We must obey God rather than men!" (Acts 5:29).

Jesus actually predicted that being his followers could get us into trouble with city hall.

> I am sending you out like sheep among wolves. There-
> fore be as shrewd as snakes and as innocent as doves.
> Be on your guard against men; they will hand you over
> to the local councils and flog you in their synagogues.
> On my account you will be brought before governors
> and kings. *Matthew 10:16-18*

Most of us who live in free societies today do not have to worry much about that sort of thing. The problem we have to reconcile more than any other is coping with various clerks and authorities who seem to love rules more than people. They appear to be incapable of making independent judgments even when the right thing to do is clearly evident. They have fallen victim to what I call "The City Hall Syndrome."

The City Hall Syndrome

We may live an exemplary home life, get along beautifully with friends and neighbors, enjoy a day of interaction at the office, feel completely at home in a world filled with all kinds of people, and still get high blood pressure whenever we have to deal with a governmental agent. There is something about working behind a counter at city hall that turns ordinarily nice people into a pain in the neck. In this chapter we will attempt to understand why such a thing happens, and look for ways to work with it and around it.

The phenomenon is not restricted to the municipal building and the courthouse. It begins to operate wherever one must work with large numbers of people who are subject to circumstantial authority. It could be an administrative office at school, a cafeteria serving line, a prison, a post office, or almost any business that has a monopoly on particular goods and services.

I bumped into it at a hospital. A year ago I became seriously ill for the first time in my life. I had pneumonia and complications. After six weeks of futile struggle with various antibiotics, the doctor said it was time to tuck me in. I arrived at the hospital feeling lousy. I was dizzy with fever, had green skin, and was frightened by the persistence of the illness and the unknowns that awaited me beyond the reception desk. I expected a nurse to rush out and start taking care of me. What I got was a blank stare from a young woman behind a computer terminal who asked me to take a seat and wait until she called my name.

When I finally got to the counter I wanted to tell her I was having difficulty breathing and that my ribs were sore where they had been touching the arms of the waiting room chair. What she wanted to know was, did I have an insurance card? Where was my place of employment? I helped her fill in the blanks. Suddenly something on the paper form was out of order. She called over another clerk and they conferred together in animated voices about what to do. I couldn't catch it all, but it went something like, "Well, you can't send him there!" "But I already have!" "You've got to change it." "But then I'll have to go into the program and change everything else." All of this exchange went on without a single reference to me as a person. No one looked up and smiled reassuringly. No one shrugged and said anything funny about detailed paperwork. I just stood there, sick and trembling, case number 913679. The experience demonstrated that the chain of modern hospital organization has two weak links. The practice of medicine, once you get in a bed, can be truly efficient and high-tech, but the front line, the reception desk, is an afterthought. The other weak link is the billing, but that is another story.

Let's try to understand. Before we become too critical of the many people whose jobs place them in public contact, we need to "wear their shoes" for a little while.

The first thing that happens is a blurring of faces. If you must spend eight hours a day selling automobile license plates to an endless line of people, they tend to lose individual character. You might sort them out into four or five types, but you can't see them as individuals. That would simply overload your circuits. It is necessary to depersonalize them. We don't look for anything unique in the individual. No doubt they represent in their persons all kinds of loves and fears, accomplishments and disasters, dreams and regrets. But we can't treat them quickly and anonymously if we get involved in that kind of distinctive information. It is also easier to be a little rude if we must in order to maintain efficiency. Managing the flow, minimizing disruptions, becomes primarily important in a human logjam.

This defense mechanism leads to the dehumanization of a large mass of people clamoring for our attention. If the people I am herding around are less than fully human, then Christ's

Golden Rule about "doing unto others" doesn't come into play.

At its extreme, some alarming atrocities have resulted. Millions of us have been systematically killed by various governments through the course of world history. The slaughter has been as heartless as that in a meat packing plant. People have been shot, hanged, poisoned, gassed, burned, drowned, and buried alive by agents working with governmental support. The grisly deeds are carried out by people who protect themselves from the stress by considering those they are murdering as somehow less than fully human. When they must defend themselves regarding such criminal behavior they say, "I was only following orders."

Anyone who has taken a course in freshman psychology is aware of the famous shock experiments conducted at Yale University in 1963. Forty males, ranging in age from twenty to fifty, responded to ads for research subjects in the field of learning and memory. All kinds of people applied. They were offered a small fee for their participation, and they could keep the money no matter what happened after they reported to the laboratory.

They were given individual appointments and told that science knew very little about the effect of punishment on learning. There was no data regarding how much punishment was best for learning. At each of these interviews an accomplice showed up pretending to be another volunteer. They drew slips of paper to see which one would be the teacher and which one would be the learner. It was rigged, of course. Both slips had "teacher" written on them. As soon as the drawing was done, they were taken to an adjacent room and the "victim" was strapped into a fake "electric chair." The experimenter explained that the straps were for his protection in case there were any muscular convulsions during the shocks. As the electrodes were applied to the "learner's" wrist, a paste was used "to prevent blisters and burns."

The real subject was then taken to a control room and told to administer a shock every time the bogus subject gave a wrong answer, moving the voltage higher each time. The teacher could not see the learner, but pounding on the wall at fake shocks above 300 volts could be heard. Obviously, there was no electricity in use at all. If the subject indicated an unwillingness to continue, the experimenter responded with a series of authoritative prods such as, "Please go on," "The experiment requires that you continue," "It is absolutely essential that you continue," "You have no other choice; you must go on." If the naive teacher asked about the dangers of the experiment he was told, "Although the shocks may be painful, there is no permanent tissue damage, so please go on."

What happened? Many subjects reacted with nervous tension, more than is usually observed in psychological testing. Subjects sweated, stuttered, trembled, groaned, bit their lips, and dug their fingernails into their flesh. Fourteen exhibited nervous laughter and smiling, even when it seemed out of place. One subject, a forty-six-year-old encyclopedia salesman, brought the experiment to a halt with a violent seizure. In later interviews these people made a big point of the fact that they did not enjoy hurting people. They were only following orders.

Not one of the forty subjects stopped advancing the supposed voltage before reaching the 300 level, at which point the victim began pounding on the wall and no longer answered the multiple-choice questions. Only fourteen of the forty (35 percent) refused to go on when told to do so by the experimenter.

Some jobs dehumanize both the "customer" and the worker. Any employment situation that rules out the expression of personal feelings or the use of unique abilities results in a loss of valuable human qualities. The only difference in the employee and a robot is that the employee needs a restroom.

The danger is particularly present for those who work in health and service professions. All day long they are thrown into situations that arouse intense emotions. Empathy can be costly. A good friend of Jesus had died. When Jesus arrived at his home, he found Lazarus' family and friends in tears. The Gospel records that "he groaned in the spirit, and was troubled" (John 11:33, KJV). People in caring professions are required to do things that are ordinarily off limits. They give the people in their care little privacy and violate their bodies with needles, enemas, and the like. Dehumanizing patients is an important coping technique. Thinking in terms of "cases" and taking a detached, objective approach is a way of preventing emotional burnout.

Being Reconciled

Do you have such a job? Government is the largest employer in the United States. Resist the temptation to dehumanize. Care about your customers. I picked up lunch at one of those fast seafood franchises. It was the height of rush hour, the line was long, and the cash register was broken. The manager had the top off of it and was talking on the telephone with a computer consultant in another city. At his elbow a little wisp of a girl was taking orders, making financial transactions on a pocket calculator, and giving continual verbal directions to the help behind the counter. When it came my turn to order, she gave no hint of stress. She gave me her full attention, looking me in the eye, smiling, and asking me what I would have. She moved smoothly through the series of questions intended to keep me from overlooking anything, gave me the total, and made change out of the register till that was on the counter in front of her. She made me feel as though I were her only customer and that everything was running exactly in order. Finishing with me, she turned to the next customer, smiled broadly and said, "May I help you?" I have never seen it done better. She was obviously enjoying her work. Dealing with the public without being defeated by broken electronics seemed to put zest in her day. She was living proof of the old adage that it is not what happens to you that matters, but how you respond to it. If you work in a job that tempts you to dehumanize the people who file past you, try giving a little extra attention to each person. It will sweeten your day as well as theirs.

While you are at it, *watch your tone of voice*. If you have to say the same thing over and over, whether on the telephone or in person, your voice can fall into a kind of sing-song tone and rhythm that can be very annoying. And watch out for an intentionally placating voice that is out of sympathy with an excited or upset person. Nothing is more irritating than a soothing voice.

The easiest way to say, "I care," even when you don't have the time to get involved, is to *actually look the other person in the eye*. Don't get lost in your terminal screen. If you are on the telephone while dealing with a live person in front of you, make it clear whether you are talking to that person or the one on the phone. Attention to little details like these will go a long way toward easing tensions in a high-pressure environment.

If you are on the receiving end, the citizen who waits your turn, there are some things you can do to help reduce the negatives that come with such encounters. For instance, try smiling. You will be amazed by how many times a smile will get you a smile in return. The hard-working person in front of you may be near the end of a difficult day. An exchange of smiles can reduce fatigue a little. It sets up the possibility for two-way caring.

Be prepared. Have your paperwork ready. Read the instructions *before* you take your place in line. Civil servants especially cannot bend rules for you—even if it means you have to make another trip on another day because you forgot a document or registration card. If you have questions, think them out ahead of time and then present them clearly and in a logical order. Sometimes it saves everybody time if you make a phone call beforehand. And don't, *don't,* burden the person behind the desk with a rundown on the numerous life tragedies that have resulted in your not having the right information or missing a deadline. Even if the person were moved to care about your problems, he or she has no power to do anything about them. If you have a complaint, take it to the appropriate office and person. True, this in itself can be a real feat on Red Tape (and Pass-the-Buck) Boulevard, but you owe it to the workers as well as those people standing in line behind you to be efficient and not make a scene—or if you do, at least make it in front of the right official.

Above all, be conscious of where you are. Learn all you can about the way business is conducted in the place where you happen to be. Social customs vary widely.

I know a man who moved to a rural county in the mountains of western Virginia. He had grown weary of the intensity of living in the metropolitan northeast. Taking his wife, three children, and a few belongings, he set off on a quest for a satisfying life of purposeful activity. That he and his family have survived the new life for a quarter of a century is evidence that he has probably found what he was looking for.

When I met him shortly after his arrival, however, he was definitely going through culture shock. The business of life was now being played out in unfamiliar dimensions where most of the rules had changed. He told me that he went into the office of the county's circuit court clerk shortly after arrival with some routine business associated with land and deeds. He said, "I spoke to her the way you have to talk to a clerk up north if you want to get attention. I wasn't angry or threatening or anything like that. Just forceful."

"And?" I asked.

"She cried!"

It will be a plus for you when you are in anonymous situations if you can say or do something that makes you unique, different from all the others. Americans are taught from childhood to "blend in," to be indistinguishable from the crowd. Our security is in being just like everyone else. We wear the right clothes, listen to the right music, drive the right cars, and generally do everything in our power to become a part of a great, grey blob of humanity. The very opposite may help you at city hall. Go ahead and be different. I once stood in line behind a man who was applying for a driver's license. When they asked him for his Social Security number he said he didn't have one. It was like a stroke of lightning. "Sir, everybody's got a Social Security number." But he didn't. Talk about individual attention! He got more than anyone else that day.

Business executives of giant corporations, diplomats, and others who might be subject to abduction in foreign countries are taking courses on how to get along with their captors. The most important single rule is to get to know your hostage-taker as a person. The more you can share about home and family, the more you can become a genuine human being, the more likely you will survive the ordeal. It is easier for one human to act aggressively toward another when little significant detail is known. It is fairly easy to strike a man if "he is an American." It becomes more difficult to abuse him if he has something in common, such as a name, an address, a sick wife, four dependent children, and an interesting hobby.

Remember that the person you are dealing with is not there to be liked. An elected official may have some sensitivities in this area, but most people working under the conditions we have outlined in this chapter cannot make any decision other than one that is strictly according to the book. The first principle of bureaucracy is *fairness*. Everyone has to be treated equally. Inconsistency at city hall will undermine the system of authority.

Most of all, be reconciled to the fact that exceptions to the rules for individuals are virtually nonexistent. Don't look for personal favors. The reply will always be the same. "Ma'am, if we let you put a live tiger in a cage on top of a five-hundred-foot tower in your back yard, everyone else will want to do it, too."

9

CHURCH FIGHTS

Christians may not see eye to eye, but they can
walk arm in arm.
Brotherhood Journal

I have an unusual avocation. I shoot public displays of
fireworks. During the time I was writing this chapter I
was sent to another city to shoot a show for Zambelli
Internationale. It takes several hours of preparation to set up
even a modest night of pyrotechnics. While I was busily tying
the fuses of the grand finale together, a police officer walked
over to me. He asked the usual string of questions. How long
have I been doing this? What are the dangers? Have I ever
been injured? Where will my next show be?

And then the policeman concluded aloud, "So this is your
only job. You do this full time."

"No, no," I corrected. "I am a Presbyterian minister. They
call me 'The Blaster Pastor'!"

He paused for about half a minute, chewing on his bottom
lip.

I thought, *Uh oh! I've scared him off.*

Then he said, "Maybe I shouldn't tell you this, but I feel like maybe the Lord sent you to me tonight."

Hey wait! I thought to myself. *I've been ordained for thirty years, and no one has ever said that to me before. I thought that was a line from religious fiction.* I made no response, continuing to load my mortars.

"I'm a close friend of our minister," he explained. "And I'm troubled. Our church is in trouble."

"Many are," I replied.

"We only have about sixty-five members. We broke off from another church."

Remaining silent, I considered how such a mix of disgruntled personalities could be a problem in itself. But then he began to talk about his friend, the minister.

"Some people are saying he has a contentious spirit. He has reported things people told him in private. He came into our Sunday school class and apologized to us. He pointed to two or three people and said he had said bad things about them. One couple got up and left. There are a lot of complaints about him."

"I can't help you much just listening to a few comments like this, but it sounds like your minister is inexperienced or immature. He is not behaving in a professional manner."

"You are right. He has only been in the ministry for six years, and he has already served five churches. He says he specializes in problem churches."

By now I had heard enough to fill in the blanks. I didn't want to discourage this nice policeman. I returned an understanding grunt.

"He said he was going to get some help from a counselor. We sort of forgave him, and then he never went."

"That sounds like the alcoholic who changes his mind about attending AA when he is sober."

"Exactly. Nobody stays in our church very long. They come a few Sundays, and then they drop out. Only a few of the charter members are still participating. Can you tell me what we ought to do?"

I did not have the opportunity to tell him anything. At that moment his portable radio came to life. Three men and two women were fighting in a discount store parking lot. He responded to the dispatcher but displayed little urgency to me. Without changing his posture he waited for me to say something. I repeated that based on his description I would conclude that his minister needed both professional education and personal counseling, adding that I really couldn't recommend anything from such a distance.

He reached into his shirt pocket and pulled out a religious tract. On its cover were the colorful fireworks of hell. "WHAT IF IT'S TRUE?" the title asked.

"Here, let me give you this. Our church name is stamped on the back." He turned toward his patrol car. "Say a prayer for us tonight."

All Churches Have Disagreements

Sometimes we dream of a perfect world, where everyone agrees, everyone shares, and everyone is kind and supportive of others. There is even an idyllic description of the early Christian church in the book of Acts.

> All the believers were together and had everything in common. Selling their possessions and goods, they gave

to anyone as he had need. Every day they continued to meet together in the temple courts. They broke bread in their homes and ate together with glad and sincere hearts, praising God and enjoying the favor of all the people. And the Lord added to their number daily those who were being saved. *Acts 2:44-47*

In a lifetime of ministry I have not yet seen such a congregation. Some function better than others. A few have developed a healthy system for maintaining voluntary associations. But all of the churches of my acquaintance have differences of opinion and dissent. No church has ever purchased a pipe organ without someone saying it would be better to send the money to the poor. No official board has ever voted to cut down a grand old tree on the church grounds without someone protesting vehemently. Paint the church and dozens will wish it were another color. Purchase new hymnbooks and some will refuse to sing. Once in a while, the congregation will get sidetracked with bickering. Rumors are flying. Fingers are pointed. Heads are wagging. A great struggle is going on.

Before we get into helpful ways to resolve church fights, let's recognize up front that a frictionless church may not be a desirable ideal. An old business adage has it that if two people agree, one of them is unnecessary. It is possible for a little conflict to be a good thing. It serves as an antidote to drowsiness and complacency. It can bring some significant issues into the foreground instead of letting them be lost in the background murmur of the organization's life.

The same book of Acts quoted above assures us that the early Christian community had its disagreements soon enough. Paul and Barnabas were a great team of missionaries. The

Bible records their adventures as they traveled around the Mediterranean preaching the Good News. One of their companions on the first missionary journey was John Mark, the author of the second Gospel. For reasons that are not explained, he turned back from the trip with Paul and Barnabas when they were in Pamphylia.

Time has passed, and Paul is ready to return to the communities where they had organized churches to see how the congregations were getting along.

> Barnabas wanted to take John, also called Mark, with them, but Paul did not think it wise to take him, because he had deserted them in Pamphylia and had not continued with them in the work. They had such a sharp disagreement that they parted company. Barnabas took Mark and sailed for Cyprus, but Paul chose Silas and left, commended by the brothers to the grace of the Lord. *Acts 15:37-40*

A Sweet Idea Turns Sour

At church we sometimes think it is "unchristian" to disagree. We are embarrassed when there is a sharp difference of opinion. I can remember being annoyed by an old minister who monopolized a regional Presbytery meeting arguing about interpretations of the *Book of Order*. I thought of him as a troublemaker who was wasting our time with his vitriolic nit-picking. I figured the Christian thing to do is to try to get along with others. Christians are supposed to be nice to each other. Church leaders ought to set the best example of caring and loving. Open conflict is a symbol of failure.

Because many church members feel this way, much unintentional damage is done. What happens is that when a few people disagree with the appropriations committee, rather than openly confront the committee they get together and hold heated private conversations about it, spreading rumors about the designs and intentions of the committee members. They may even circulate a letter expressing their discontent, not to the entire congregation, but to a selected group of addresses.

A common, yet destructive, approach of many disgruntled church members is the secret meeting. Like-minded people gather at someone's home or in the church parking lot. Rumors fly. People who are not present to defend themselves are chopped to ribbons. This hidden, underground dissension is a clear indicator of a congregation with an unhealthy problem. The waste in all of this is that the problem itself is never dealt with. The people responsible for the dissatisfaction are kept in the dark. Secret meetings are in a class with anonymous letters; they both belong in the garbage.

When conflict is kept behind closed doors it will lengthen the time it takes to resolve it, and it increases the possibility of upheaval. Talk will turn to pinning the blame and getting rid of someone. Whenever such activity takes place without everyone being informed and invited, serious trouble is not far away.

There are two distinct ways to deal with church fights. One is to view it as a contest in which there are winners and losers. The other is to see it as a problem to be solved. It doesn't take much thought to see that the latter approach is the healthiest in most situations. Perhaps there can be gains for both sides that will enhance the good of all. This way will take more care and attention, of course.

When dealing with church fights it is important to establish some common goals and find ways to get there. Until this is done, the congregation will be like the man who jumped on a horse and rode off in all directions. It is absolutely necessary to see beyond any given contest to the purposes and dreams of the group as a whole. Members in any church will find healthy empowerment when they find a way to work together to achieve valuable goals they can agree on. Working independently in little cliques resolves nothing.

Some Facts about Churches

Church membership is the prime example of voluntary association. People join particular churches because they want to be there. There is something about that church that meets a personal need. Ministers like to believe the primary need that is being met is spiritual. Church members like the preaching, the Bible study, the prayer services, the fellowship, the missionary outreach. For many, that may be the case. But a decision to join and remain a part of a congregation is a complex and poorly understood behavior. For some, it could be political power. They come on board with an eye to serving on committees and rising to positions of authority and leadership. For others, it may be a desire to mix with the "right" people. Church members could be excellent customers, clients, and partners. Still others may have an overwhelming need for "warm fuzzies" and are seeking acceptance, hugs, praise, and a couple of hours of fun to highlight an otherwise bland week. We are complex, and the motivations for seeking out (or leaving) a particular congregation are equally complex.

Every church must maintain itself or die. Sure, there are a few small rural congregations that receive mission support from the denomination, but in today's economy these are becoming the exception to the rule. Staff salaries must be paid, necessary repairs to the property cannot be put off forever, bills arrive regularly, and there is always the necessity of addressing the needs of those who are not members of the congregation. All this takes money, and unless somebody is bankrolling the whole enterprise it requires the freely given contributions of the membership. One way members express their satisfaction or dissatisfaction with their church is through their financial contributions. Refusing to pledge, or reducing the amount placed in the offering plate is a common way of participating in a church fight.

Everyone Welcome is a motto seen on many church signs. That probably is not true. People are different. There are many varieties of religious expression. What is pleasing to one may be disturbing to another. Many are thoroughly satisfied with formal ritual. Others prefer a looser, more spontaneous church experience. Some Christians are emphatic about soul-winning; others are more into social justice. The various churches in a community may worship the same God and read the same Bible, but they present a rich variety of emphasis and behavior. There is nothing wrong with this. Those who dream of a "united" Christian church somewhere in the future, when Jesus finally heals all of our divisions, will simply have to reckon with the fact that even that great church will have to allow for many different cultural tastes and needs.

If this is true, then "everyone" will simply never feel welcomed at any particular church. It will be unrealistic to imagine that everyone in town can be attracted to a particular congregation. Some will join prematurely only to discover later that they do not exactly fit. There is no fight, as such, going on when a few people decide a certain congregation is not where they feel at home. It will be better for them, and better for the identity of the particular church, if they find a more appropriate place in which to participate.

The significant fact to keep in mind about all church life is that *everyone wants to matter.* Even the sporadic "pew warmer" who never gets into the heavy demands of committee work needs to feel important and respected. A lack of recognition is at the root of many church fights. Depression results when we feel we can't make a difference. An entire congregation can become depressed for this reason. The leadership of such a church needs to let its members understand that there are ways they can be heard, ways they can change things through the system. What we need when we are in voluntary associations are experiences of some kind of encouraging success. We need visible evidence that church life can be inspiring and meaningful.

The Anatomy of Church Fights

Paul wrote to the church he had organized in Corinth,

> I am afraid that when I come I may not find you as I want you to be, and you may not find me as you want me to be. I fear that there may be quarrreling, jealousy, outbursts of anger, factions, slander, gossip, arrogance and disorder. *2 Corinthians 12:20*

Church fights vary in their degree of intensity and threat to the well-being of the organization. At the mildest level it may be little more than an animated discussion or debate. Some issue has caught the interest and imagination of a few people, who begin wagging their tongues about it. Almost anything can set it off, especially if it's new. It might be the pastor's choice of cars or the shape of the offering envelopes. The object of this kind of conversation may be as innocent as someone noticing that the speaker is observant and concerned. Even at its most heated little more is sought than having the listener nod in agreement.

Sometimes these strongly opinionated discourses take place on church property. Kitchens and parking lots are common spots. If the subject is colorful enough they may occur far away from the shadow of the steeple. I have overheard them in barber shops, supermarkets, sports stadiums, and around backyard barbecue grills.

At the next level of seriousness the participants are looking for a clear win, which is to say, someone must lose. The contest remains "friendly" in the sense that rival football teams understand they are just playing a game. In fact, it is desirable to have a worthy opponent. I watched two boxers slugging it out in the tenth round. They were giving it all they had and the crowd was going wild. No one went down, and when the bell rang to end the fight, the two boxers touched gloves and hugged each other in an expression of respect and gratitude. "You gave me a good fight," they seemed to be saying. "I may have a bruised chin, but this was better than coming in here and taking out some stiff who doesn't know how to defend himself."

Game-playing, even on this rougher level, is not threatening to a church's health. It might even be a little invigorating. No harm comes from an exchange of views or an expression of opinion that may not be popular. Perhaps the point is valid.

Maybe there is something worthwhile to be discovered in a minority report. If the rules are being followed, if there is an agreed-upon order of authority, if everyone involved senses that there is truly an opportunity to be heard and responded to, then nothing is out of control. The process is healthy, if noisy, and it will lead to some kind of consensus and eventual ownership by everyone.

Difficulty arises when the dispute leads to open conflict. It is one thing to try to persuade someone else to agree with you; it is something else to threaten to take your marbles and go home if you don't succeed. Harm begins when an antagonist goes for the jugular vein of an opponent, questioning that person's right to participate, calling names, and putting down people in positions of responsibility. At this level there is disruption. Now people are being hurt. My mother sang alto in the church choir. I remember the night she came home from choir practice in tears. Another singer had said she had a vibrato like a billy goat.

Somewhere along the way, the minister, the musician, the official board, the church secretary, or a committee chairman will be challenged by some members who have a need to prove themselves. Sickness comes to the church body when the remarks are no longer made to be helpfully instructive but are sharpened in order to injure, embarrass, or annihilate a target. Stable relationships become shaky. No one knows for sure who can be trusted. Friendships are threatened. People are taking sides. There may be two sides, or there may be three or four sides. The word *split* begins to turn up in conversations. The fight has become a deadly war.

Quitting is an indicator that things are reaching the critical stage. It may be that an individual or several families who were once "regulars" begin to skip worship services. A church officer once told me that things "got so bad around there" that he and his family would drive out into the country on Sunday mornings rather than go to church. He said, "If we went, we would feel the tension the whole time, and when we went home we would feel bad." On another level, a leader may not attend a particular meeting or may walk out when the debate gets too heavy.

All the reasons for fighting we discovered in the first chapter apply to church fights. Sex, territory, power, boredom, and frustration are all active in God's house. Sometimes, as horrifying as it may be to find such a motive in church, it is pure revenge. Someone wants to even a score: "He hurt me, and I am going to hurt him."

Being Reconciled Together

What can you do when your church is experiencing destructive conflict? If you are the minister, the answer is discouraging: You are too close to the situation. Your salary is paid by this congregation. It is highly probable that you are what the struggle is all about. Every minister has members who are dissatisfied, who don't receive enough attention, who disagree with things that are said in sermons, and who are annoyed by "the way things are going." They may represent 2 percent of the congregation or 75 percent. You may never know. You may have a close group of supporters who think you walk on water, but the others are there. If you know who they are, you might win over two or three of them by giving them an extraordinary amount of attention, but you will never win them all. Many will quietly put up with you, waiting for the day a new minister arrives who may give them more of what they need. There is little way, then, for a minister to personally manage church conflict.

The best thing to do is to design a clean, honest, open system through which the members can work out their own problems without coming to blows. If this fails, about the only hope (short of divine intervention) is to secure the services of an outsider, a consultant with some expertise in resolving church fights. It can help to have an "audience" present. A third party not involved in the contest can defuse the situation. We do not fight very well in public. An impartial, neutral observer at an emotional meeting can have a dampening effect on the open expression of hostility. Most of all, such a person can help us examine where we have been and what we are doing in a way that brings healing insight. After listening to all sides, a summary of what has been heard can be surprisingly helpful in many situations. The Alban Institute is the nation's leading organization serving this purpose. Their telephone number is listed in the appendix.

It is important for a church to take action quickly. Don't wait for emotions to overflow and interfere with clear thinking. Brush fires are more easily extinguished than forest fires. If people in conflict avoid each other, there is no chance for improvement. If they lock horns the minute they meet instead of nibbling away at the difficulty a little bit at a time, there will be a lot of anger followed by withdrawal and separation. Few church fights can ever be solved at one meeting. Work on it slowly, deliberately, incrementally.

I can think of no instance in the Gospels where Jesus ever avoided conflict. His disciples begged him not to go into

Jerusalem on Palm Sunday. Nothing but trouble waited for him there.

> They were on their way up to Jerusalem, with Jesus leading the way, and the disciples were astonished, while those who followed were afraid. Again he took the Twelve aside and told them what was going to happen to him. "We are going up to Jerusalem," he said, "and the Son of Man will be betrayed to the chief priests and teachers of the law. They will condemn him to death and will hand him over to the Gentiles, who will mock him and spit on him, flog him and kill him." *Mark 10:32-34*

There are some helpful things that can be done to restore unity in a congregation that is at odds with itself. Look for solutions that will satisfy as many people as possible. It is entirely possible that if the people involved will prayerfully seek a way to resolve the contest, one will be found. Each one will not be *totally* satisfied. Everyone may have to give up a little something. It will be worth the cost if the result is a mutually acceptable resolution of the issue.

One of the antique vows for officers in my denomination used to be to promise "subjection to the brethren in the Lord." This one has been dropped, but the idea behind it remains helpful. In modern terms it could be an affirmation of "the loyal opposition." It is possible to disagree with an action by an official board without getting bent out of shape. I was once part of a commission sent in to help resolve a difficulty at a neighboring church. I will never forget a comment made by one of the church officers. "We may disagree," he said, "but we are united." There is room in any healthy church for differences of opinion.

When script writers are running out of time for the resolution of plot problems, they let the hero draw a gun and shoot the villain. The movie way of solving problems is not very practical in churches. Responsible leaders should be quick to point out that stinging comments and driving someone away are not positive actions. It is far better to find a way to change a pattern of behavior than to get rid of the person. *All of us can learn new lessons*. We can improve the way we do things. Even the ones upon whom the burden of correction falls can maintain a sense of humility before God. "Brothers, if someone is caught in a sin, you who are spiritual should restore him gently. But watch yourself, or you also may be tempted" (Galatians 6:1).

Go back and read chapter 7 again. Everything that is said there about negotiation and management of conflict is useful among volunteers at church. Keep in mind that your group will need to reach a recognizable decision. Reconciliation will occur on no other grounds. It can't be put off indefinitely. There will come a time when everyone involved must vote for or against the proposed solution. Someone needs to ring a bell and end the fight. Dragging it out longer will only increase the alienation and antagonism.

Sometimes there will simply have to be clear winners and losers. In some situations painful confrontation can't be avoided. Circumstances force a showdown. The important thing for the church is that such a conflict be conducted in a manner that is fair to all sides. An open, democratic process becomes important and life-saving.

A Helpful Guide

In 1992 the 204th General Assembly of the Presbyterian Church produced some "Guidelines for Presbyterians During Times of Disagreement." It can be of great value to any congregation, regardless of denomination.

In a spirit of trust and love, we promise each other that we will:

1. Treat each other respectfully so as to build trust, believing that we all desire to be faithful to Jesus Christ:

   - We will keep our conversations and communications open for candid and forthright exchange.

   - We will not ask questions or make statements in a way that will intimidate or judge others.

2. Share our concerns directly with individuals or groups with whom we have disagreements in a spirit of love and respect in keeping with Jesus' teaching.

3. Focus on ideas and suggestions instead of questioning people's motives, intelligence, or integrity; we will not engage in name-calling or labeling of others prior to, during, or following the discussion.

4. Learn about various positions on the topic of disagreement.

5. State what we think we heard and ask for clarification before responding, in an effort to be sure we understand each other.

6. Indicate where we agree with those of other viewpoints as well as where we disagree.

7. Share our personal experiences about the subject of disagreement so that others may more fully understand our concerns.

8. Seek to stay in community with each other though the discussion may be vigorous and full of tension; we will be ready to forgive and be forgiven.

9. Follow these additional guidelines when we meet in decision-making bodies:

   - Urge persons of various points of view to speak and promise to listen to these positions seriously.

   - Seek conclusions informed by our points of agreement.

   - Be sensitive to the feelings and concerns of those who do not agree with the majority and respect their rights of conscience.

   - Abide by the decision of the majority, and if we disagree with it and wish to change it, work for that change in ways that are consistent with these guidelines.

10. Include our disagreements in our prayers, not praying for triumph of our viewpoints, but seeking God's grace to listen attentively, to speak clearly, and to remain open to the vision God holds for us all.

Reprinted from "Seeking to Be Faithful Together: Guidelines for Presbyterians During Times of Disagreement." This paper was adopted by the 204th General Assembly 1992 Presbyterian Church (U.S.A.). Used by permission of the Presbyterian Peacemaking Program, 100 Witherspoon Street, Louisville, Kentucky 40202.

10

HUGGING GOD

When I am with God
My fear is gone
In the great quiet of God.
My troubles are as the pebbles on the road,
My joys are like the everlasting hills.
Walter Rauschenbusch, *The Little Gate to God*

D o you love God? That is a far more important question than "Do you believe in God?" The question of belief has too many catches to be worthwhile. Are you asking me if I accept your understanding of God? Does that mean you have completely identified the fullness of the Divine Nature and cataloged all the height, breadth, and depth of the Eternal and understand exactly what it is that is being done for us and is expected of us in return?

Isn't it a basic truth that God is bigger than our best thoughts about him? Doesn't he, by nature, exceed our wildest imagination? If this is true, then the God we define is not God. The God we are so confident we know is not the fullness of God.

The theological task we think we have concluded is but a finite beginning of an effort to unravel an infinite problem. The simple system of faith and salvation we have worked out so neatly may satisfy us at one stage in our spiritual development, but it will not do for a lifetime, and it certainly can't be expected to answer the spiritual longings of everyone else.

The Bible wastes no time arguing and proving the existence of God. Of course God exists. Most people will agree with that until you start turning God into the exclusive property of your denomination, cult, or classroom. The significant question is: What do you think of God? How do you conceive him? Is the God of your experience lovable? What images, feelings, responses do you have when the subject of God is brought to your attention?

Beginners are likely to get stuck with a "vague, oblong blur." They haven't spent enough time with the Bible or darkened enough church doors to refine their thoughts about God. At the other extreme, professionally religious people may have passed through living faith into a kind of spiritual numbness. Handling holy things intimately so much of the time, they have lost all traces of awe and reverence. Professors of systematic theology carry a special kind of spiritual handicap.

What Is God Like?

Many Christians think God is angry with them. They feel alienated from God. They try to do things to earn God's love. They work hard to prove their worthiness. Some even attempt (perhaps subconsciously) to buy God's favor through sacrificial offerings and marathon committee work. The idea seems to be that God won't forgive us unless we appease him. God is like a crotchety old grandfather who has to be placated if we want to inherit anything. Most of the people who think about God in these terms will deny it. In fact, they will become angry with what they think is an unfair caricature of their theological system. But as I listen to a lot of popular religious teaching I can only conclude that the "caricature" is accurate. And that's a pity.

The New Testament calls us to "be reconciled to God" (2 Corinthians 5:20). That's something like giving God a hug. How can we do that? Through Christ. God reveals himself to us in Jesus. In the life of Christ we can see God pleading with us to be reconciled to him. "God is love" (1 John 4:16). When we recognize God in Christ, those dark, angry, threatening ideas of God become intolerable; they no longer line up.

Jesus did not change God's attitude toward us when he died on the cross. He died on the cross because God already loved us. It was God's great affection for this world that sent his Son here to be with us.

If we think of Christ's activity as reconciling an angry God, it is as though he were a third party, a negotiator of the sort we have discussed in earlier chapters. Jesus stands between us and God and helps us to "kiss and make up." This is a popular teaching, and it is simply mistaken. God is not the object of Jesus' reconciling act. If it were that way, our salvation would have been negotiated by a broker. It would have been bought and paid for. The religious imagery of Christ paying our debt of sin has its roots in the Bible, but we are led astray by the way it is commonly interpreted today. The one unavoidable aspect of God's grace is that it can't be bought. Not by us. Not by Jesus. God's love is not for sale. It is a gift, freely given to unworthy people. We may sing "He purchased my pardon on Calvary's tree," but it is a crude metaphor for the Christian understanding of reconciliation.

Do you remember what we learned in chapter 2? *God* does this thing. *He* is the prime mover. Reconciliation is the result of *his* love for us. It is his gift to us. *Gratis*. There can be no such thing as a negotiated grace. The words cancel each other out. Sooner could there be a squared circle than purchased love. Yes, Jesus is our mediator. But this is not how his mediation works. God doesn't need to be mollified. Jesus doesn't make God stop being angry with us. A loving God is in Christ. There are not three parties at work. There are two: God and us.

Are you reconciled to God? Do you love him? Would you run from him and hide if you saw him coming, or would you throw your arms around him and hug him if you could? This is the most crucial question we will ever be asked.

Barriers

Admittedly, our experience of human life provides us with many opportunities to question the love of God. I was talking with a man whose mother had died. "I can accept this more gracefully," he said. "She had lived a full life. But when my father died I was angry. I mean, he had worked hard all his life. For what? He was entitled to some pleasant years of retirement. I couldn't understand why God would take him so soon."

The volume of human tragedy in the world is vastly beyond our comprehension. We are moved by television images of starving children in Somalia or weeping widows in Croatia, but the sad people in those pictures are an immeasurable fraction of the total burden of human suffering at any given moment. Most of it seems to be random, without reason or justification. In the Old Testament, Job's friends were sure he was being punished for some unconfessed sin, but the whole point of the book is that Job was blameless. How can a loving God permit evil in the world, hypocrisy in the church, random tragedy, sickness and death?

There are no easy explanations. Trusting faith is our only recourse. And yet it is precisely among the ranks of the troubled and suffering that the most solidly supportive faith can be found. There is apparently a gift of understanding and acceptance that is denied to those of us who remain on the outside, looking in.

Regardless of our personal acquaintance with suffering, there is a difference between accepting God in Christ and being fully reconciled to God. Whether we grow up in a Christian home absorbing faith in God almost by osmosis, or have a dramatic conversion experience as an adult, this awakening of the soul is only the beginning. The nurturing of that elemental faith is something that continues for a lifetime. As our faith matures we have less difficulty with unanswerable questions about barriers to belief in a loving God. Job, in the depth of personal tragedy, said, "Though he slay me, yet will I trust him" (Job 13:15, KJV).

The Essence of Christianity

Some teachers of the law asked Jesus to single out the most important of all the Commandments. Without hesitation our Lord quoted the great *Shema Israel* that is recorded in the sixth chapter of Deuteronomy.

"The most important one," answered Jesus, "is this: 'Hear O Israel, the Lord our God, the Lord is one. *Love* the Lord your God with all your heart and with all your soul and with all your mind and with all your strength.'" *Mark 12:29-30*

Notice I emphasized the word *love*. That is what is asked of us by the greatest commandment of them all. We are to love God.

Now what do we do with that? Is it enough to love generic ideas like truth and righteousness? Does loving God mean attending worship and doing the things we believe God wants us to do? Think about it! Being good and honest are not the same thing as loving God for who God is. Going to church regularly, as desirable as that is, can hardly be a substitute for loving God with our whole heart, soul, mind, and strength.

God wants our love. The Bible leaves no doubt about that. He wishes we would "hug" him. So many Christians in good standing who have faith in God and try to do his will have somehow missed the fact that the first thing required of us is that we love him.

If you will read your Bible you will notice that the God who is active among people on this earth is far from a vague concept of the holy. He is quite the opposite of a blur. The Yahweh who dealt so firmly with Moses is not an abstraction. He is a person. He is the "one." When Jesus made this same God known to us as "our Father," he underscored the personal, individual, lovable nature of God.

The Scriptures assure us over and over again that God loves us, and that he loves us in spite of our unloveliness. We don't deserve it, but for reasons of his own God cares about us, grieves when we grieve, is glad when we are glad. A mother once said to me, "When everything is all right with the children, everything is all right." And that's the way it is with God. This is the most remarkable thing we can find in the Bible. God loves us even though we are sinners, and he deeply desires our love in return.

It is simply inconceivable that God, who has revealed himself to us in Jesus Christ as "Father," could be content with our respect and obedience without love. God is love, and love passionately seeks a response in love. Nothing less will satisfy.

Keeping Love Alive

For some reason, first-generation Christians tend to love God more openly than fourth- or fifth-generation Christians. New churches in developing nations are alive with the enthusiasm and fervor of people who have made a fresh discovery. In the United States and Europe many "mainline" denominations are struggling to stay awake. There are exceptional congregations here and there, and a change for the better seems to be on the horizon, but overall statistics have been discouraging.

The Old Testament reminds us that the descendants of those Israelites who conquered the Promised Land with God's help not only stopped loving God, but actually turned their backs on him. Bible interpreters explain it as a social phenomenon. The Jews who settled down in villages and practiced agriculture felt different from the Jews who were wandering shepherds or former slaves looking for a home. The God of the desert nomads seemed irrelevant to homeowners and gardeners. They were naturally attracted to Baal, the god of fertility. It wasn't long before Yahweh was a dim memory.

The annual Passover celebration was intended to remind everyone of the way God rescued them from slavery in Egypt—a
good reason for loving God. Passover was kept, year after
year, but people lost sight of its meaning. They ceased to love
God.

Jesus tells us the same thing can happen among his followers.

> At that time many will turn away from the faith and will
> betray and hate each other, and many false prophets
> will appear and deceive many people. Because of the
> increase of wickedness, the love of most will grow cold.
> *Matthew 24:10-12*

The Christian celebration of the Lord's Supper is intended
to remind us of God's love for us in Christ's sacrifice on the
cross. In the church I serve, we have Communion once a
month. Some churches observe it every Sunday. When I stayed
with some monks in a monastery, mass was celebrated every
morning. It is a reminder of how much reason we have to
love God. Still, our love grows cold.

The New Testament tells us God has promised the crown
of life and the kingdom to "those who love him" (James 1:12;
2:5). Being reconciled to God, loving God, is at the very heart
of Christianity. The textbooks speak of "salvation by faith
alone" as opposed to "salvation by works," but I have yet to
see any mention of salvation by love.

A Pharisee invited Jesus to dinner. We make a mistake
when we think of a Pharisee as a bad person. True, they don't
get very good press in the New Testament, but they were
among the community's best citizens. They were God-fearing,

law-abiding, church-supporting, do-everything-right kind of people. They were utterly dependable. Nice people. Good neighbors.

> When a woman who had lived a sinful life in that town learned that Jesus was eating at the Pharisee's house, she brought an alabaster jar of perfume, and as she stood behind him at his feet weeping, she began to wet his feet with her tears. Then she wiped them with her hair, kissed them and poured perfume on them. *Luke 7:37-38*

The Pharisee was disgusted by this woman's presence and behavior. After telling him a parable about forgiveness Jesus said,

> "Do you see this woman? I came into your house. You did not give me any water for my feet, but she wet my feet with her tears and wiped them with her hair. You did not give me a kiss, but this woman, from the time I entered, has not stopped kissing my feet. You did not put oil on my head, but she has poured perfume on my feet. Therefore, I tell you, her many sins have been forgiven—for she loved much. But he who has been forgiven little loves little." *Luke 7:44-47*

There can be no doubt that being reconciled with others is the first step we can take in the life of faith. The ultimate step, however, is being reconciled to God. *And when we are reconciled to God we will love God.* We will love him with all our heart, soul, mind, and strength.

A gentleman approached me with a very intense expression on his face one Sunday after worship. "I have difficulty," he said, "trying to be intimate with God. Every notion I have about God is so overwhelming and abstract. I just can't seem to get on friendly, personal terms with the Almighty."

He was quite sincere, searching my face for some kind of an answer.

"It's difficult for a lot of people," I assured him. "Maybe that's why God sent his son. Jesus said, 'Anyone who has seen me has seen the Father' (John 14:9). I don't think it would violate his meaning if we extended that to imply, 'When you love me, you are loving the Father.'"

11

DIFFICULT CASES

Being all fashioned of the self-same dust,
Let us be merciful as well as just.
Henry Wadsworth Longfellow: *Tales of a Wayside Inn,
Part III*

Not every conflict can be resolved. You will get into fights that defy your best intentions. There are situations where it is essentially impossible for you to do anything to make things better. You will simply have to learn to go on living. Remember, way back in chapter 2 we saw that the scriptural injunction is, *"If it is possible, as far as it depends on you,* live at peace with everyone" (Romans 12:18). God knows it is not always possible. Sometimes your best efforts and intentions are met with continued hostility and aggression.

Our world has a heavy population of people who are functioning well enough to survive, but who are crippled by what may be termed a "character disorder." They are difficult to live with. We are not thinking here of serious psychiatric abnormalities. In these milder instances there is no distortion of reality, no uncontrollable anxiety, no psychopathic inability to distinguish between right and wrong, and no disability because of brain damage. We are thinking about "ordinary" people who have perfected a way of dealing with others and their own emotions that interferes with the establishment of lasting relationships. Their own feelings inside themselves are distorted. They look at the world and the people in it and perceive something different from what most of us see.

As troubling as they are, they are not a threat to society. We don't need to lock them up for our safety. They don't have an illness with symptoms that can be treated with medicine or therapy. What they have is a peculiar way of thinking and a special set of feelings toward other people. Most people with character disorders are quite pleased with themselves. They may be a frustration and a discomfort to the people around them, but their self-image is positive. Far from hurting inside, they have become so secure in their character style that you will find them extremely resistant to change. In fact, the things in their behavior that annoy us have become essential to their sense of well-being.

Many of us are not able to cope effectively with some rough experiences as we are growing up. Consequently, our personalities can develop gaps of impaired functioning. All children learn various strategies for evading painful emotional stresses. These defense strategies allow us to manipulate others into supporting us in areas where we feel inadequate. Most of all, these patterns become ways to avoid personal emotional pain.

This chapter reviews *in nontechnical terms* some of the most common character disorders. There are no secret tricks you can bring into play when you attempt to reconcile a difference with such personalities. The best that can be done is to equip yourself with understanding in order to avoid some obvious traps. You have not lost when you are defeated by these.

Paranoia

This term became popular years ago when Humphrey Bogart rolled those steel ball bearings around in his hands while on trial in "The Caine Mutiny." Today it is the subject of popular songs. Remember, we are thinking here not about a mental illness, but about a highly developed way of defensive thinking. At its extreme, paranoia becomes a psychosis, producing classic symptoms of persecution or grandeur. A few paranoiacs become murderers. Many enjoy futile litigation in court. The everyday experiences you have with mild paranoia are not that dramatic. These neighbors, church members, relatives, customers, and fellow workers you regularly have to deal with don't carry elaborate delusions about the world. What gives them a problem is that they distort the significance of what they see in you and others. This makes them a problem for you. They become general nuisances, quarrelling with and falsely accusing most of the people who come into their lives.

The paranoiacs you may face every day have a fear of their own emotions. They have learned to expect trouble every time they become happy, sad, angry, sexually aroused, or whatever. They don't want to look like fools. Expressing their feelings exposes them to risks of injury. Driven by fear, they force their emotions into submission. They don't do a lot of laughing, crying, or playing. Their words and actions are carefully planned rather than spontaneous.

The basic tool of paranoia is projection. They take the things they feel and pin them on others. They think everyone else is just like they are. I once sat on a review board that had to make a difficult decision about the suitability of a certain individual to be in the ministry. When he sat down at the table with us he said, "I sense a lot of hostility in this room."

Projection is almost impossible to correct. The more you discuss it the more the one projecting is threatened. A deeper and firmer position is taken on each round of questioning. Everything you say confirms the paranoiac's suspicion that you are out to get him or her.

If you want to get along with a person who has groomed a paranoid way of thinking, don't expect any changes. Marriage and having children will not change them. Friendship will make no dent in their defenses. Instead of trying to remake a personality, attempt to determine which emotions are most threatening to that person. Then try to avoid any provocations in that area. Enjoy those feelings yourself without demanding the other to join you.

Obsession and Compulsion

The obligation of duty weighs heavily on some people. They feel pressured to do better work in less time. They may tell you their boss, spouse, teacher, or whoever expects superhuman performance from them, but it is likely they are pushing themselves.

You will find an obsessive/compulsive person to be inflexible. Their rigidity makes creative spontaneity a rare occurrence. Routine is what brings security. They meticulously plan their daily lives, and they become irritated when anything disrupts their set pattern. They are hard workers who are not easily distracted by activity around them. There is little room in their day for recreation or friendly banter.

Driven by the thought, *I must,* an obsessive/compulsive personality can get caught up in endless housecleaning, computing, golfing, or whatever. By staying busy they can escape all kinds of troubling thoughts and human encounters. "He is preoccupied," we explain.

Again, this behavior is not ordinarily unhealthy or neurotic. The individuals you deal with who are obsessive/compulsive will be reliable, punctual, conscientious, and completely trustworthy with all the details. In all probability the people who proofread this book and put it on these pages have a degree of obsessive/compulsive behavior. That's why they are good at what they do. The same applies to clerical workers and accountants. Far from being a handicap, profound attention to detail is required. Science would not be where it is today if such people did not exist.

Perhaps you are more familiar with obsessive/compulsive behavior than you think. Have you ever known a child to object when someone skipped a sentence in a familiar book? Did you ever try to avoid stepping on sidewalk cracks or walking under a ladder? Have you ever washed your hands in a public restroom and then wondered if you needed to wash them again after turning off the spigot? Have you made a ritual of brushing your teeth or putting on your shoes? All these little ceremonies fall into this category. They are not harmful and do not prevent us from living productive lives.

The possibility of conflict with an obsessive/compulsive personality is always quite likely for the simple reason that they are disturbed when you interrupt their rigid routine. Perhaps you are a church usher and you take someone to the wrong seat. Or maybe you decide to put some flowers on the right side of a table when they have always gone on the left. Your offense could be more serious, such as arriving home late for dinner or forgetting to check in by phone. Buying a new house or remodelling an existing one may bring surprising grief.

There is not much you can do to repair this kind of brokenness. Your only recourse is a warm, patient love for the other person. Once comfortable routine is reestablished the upset will become history.

Hysteria

The term *hysteria* derives from the Greek word for "womb" that is at the root of "hysterectomy." Many years ago it was assumed that hysteria was a female disorder. When Freud told the Vienna Medical Society in 1886 that men could also be hysterical it was considered nonsense.

Some words psychiatrists throw around have many meanings. Hysteria is one of the broadest of them all. It is used to cover a variety of neurological disturbances as well as other conditions, such as twilight states and amnesia. Popular usage applies it to the overly dramatic behavior (histrionics) so common in movie scripts. Here, we are thinking only about hysteria as a character disorder. It is an unfortunate term for this use, but so far no one has come up with a better one. Unlike paranoia and obsessive/compulsive behavior, this kind of hysteria doesn't "get worse." There is absolutely no connection here with the other problems that take the same name. Think of hysteria as a set of personality characteristics including naiveté and emotional immaturity with a defensive style of denial and repression. It can be called an "anxiety reaction" or a "phobic (fear) reaction."

An extreme example of an anxiety reaction is commonplace in combat. Talk with any veteran of a shooting war and you will hear about soldiers who became paralyzed with fear and were unable to fire a weapon. Such hysteria often takes away all feeling in hands and arms. In all the great wars clever doctors had to find ways to restore the victim's sense of touch. One therapy that worked was asking the patients to draw the abnormal state of unfeelingness off like a glove, an inch or two a day, removing it entirely just before they were discharged for home.

The hysterics we are likely to disturb in ordinary living are people who repress any emotion that may conflict with their mood of the moment. They perceive the world around them through a lens colored by their feelings of the moment. This blurs a lot of reality. They seemed starved for affection. They need a lot of attention and approval. They make many demands on others. When you finally get them off the phone you feel drained.

Children discover how to get attention by being hysterical. Some keep it up for a lifetime. By adolescence a few discover they can get the attention they need by being sexually seductive. An insecure child in an adult body is desperate for love and approval. They rarely have any genuine interest in sex but tend to play at it, sometimes bringing disaster to themselves and others.

Don't let hysterics mislead you. It may be that the big flap that caught you by surprise and seems so irreconcilable is little more than a plea for love and security. You can't do much good during the height of the conflict. Later, when things have cooled a bit, giving some attention can be healing.

Emotional Immaturity

Many of the troublesome personalities you will encounter are manifestations of emotional immaturity. The passing of years is not enough in itself to produce a genuine adult. All of us learn little ways to deal with others that produce the kind of results we prefer. Most of us change our technique as we progress through our "formative years." Some of us get stuck. If the behavior pattern works when we are five we figure it ought to do equally well when we are fifty. We don't bother to experiment with other ways of relating with people. Here is a list of seven immature emotional techniques or styles. All of them are disordered. The people who use them do not often have lasting relationships with others and tend to think poorly of themselves.

Temperamental

A temperamental person bounces from happiness to sadness like a tennis ball in play. Little time is spent near the net. Most of their feelings are at the extremes. Sensitivity runs high. "She wears her feelings on her sleeve," we say. A temperamental person's responses are very unpredictable, which means that people around him or her are kept off balance.

Trying to be reconciled with a temperamental person is somewhat like attempting to inflate a tire with a nail in it. There will be some gain, some loss—mostly loss. It's important that you avoid getting caught in their emotional trap with them. If they are depressed, they will try to depress you. Resist this at all costs. Laugh at them and tell them they are being silly. The real person is actually there somewhere near the tennis net and not out there on the line the way his or her behavior indicates. It is not likely that temperamental people are either as wretched or as noble as they say they are.

A temperamental person is an emotional black hole. He or she will consume all their own reserves and then try to suck in all the life around them in an effort to sustain the extreme good or bad feeling. Don't become a victim. If you can't change the subject, hang up and call back later or walk away until the climate has changed.

There is one serious caution. Sometimes a "temperamental" individual may be on a medication that creates these problems as a side effect. Many of the wrongly named "recreational drugs" can do this as well. Bipolar and unipolar disorders are also rampant in our society today, causing enormous suffering that is beyond the patient's ability to control by will power alone. When you think you may be having difficulty with someone who is merely temperamental, allow for these significant other possibilities. You may never know all the facts about these things.

Explosive

Some people have the disposition of a grizzly bear or a snapping turtle. They respond to your approach with sudden outbursts of rage. Often you will have no idea what you have done to trigger the explosion. It is somewhat like patting people on their shoulders as a gesture of friendliness and having them cringe because under their shirt they are sun-burned, and you didn't know it. An office worker crossed the hall and asked a secretary a simple question. The answer was a violent, "Don't ask me! They never tell me anything around here!"

This behavior (which is closely related to the temperamental personality described above) might be the result of medication or alcohol abuse. Sometimes people with short emotional fuses will turn to drugs in an effort to control their outbursts. The resulting behavior spiral becomes tighter with the passage of time, and the attempt to help themselves turns into a damaging addiction. The outbursts become even more furious.

Explosive personalities may seem self-assured and in control, but they are usually unhappy with themselves. They need your friendship more than they can say. To be reconciled to such a person, affirm who they are when they are not blowing off steam. A forgiving spirit on your part can help. But don't take too much risk! Don't allow yourself to become a punching bag. If you are being abused, you are not doing yourself or the other person any good. See the appendix for some guidelines on this.

Manipulative

A manipulative person is simply not interested in making up with you. He or she has no desire for a close relationship. Somewhere along the way manipulative persons have probably been hurt by parental rejection. Their experience of warm, accepting love is near zero. They have stopped looking for it.

They don't think they need it. Instead of becoming interested in people they make close ties with things. They substitute a love affair with wealth, power, success, and fame for close companionship with others. People become objects from which things are acquired.

You will have plenty of association with manipulative persons. What you will notice is that they are not able to share your feelings about anything. They have little sense of guilt. They smooth their method of dealing with others only as a way to get what they want out of them. They are masters of deception.

Manipulative persons are as resistant to change as a pig is to cleanliness. They will drop you long before they decide to live differently. Since their emotions are fairly invulnerable to pain, they have little desire to change. These will be some of your most difficult challenges. They are not likely to participate in any act of reconciliation. Don't expect too much of them. They will take advantage of you. They can be something like pet panthers, purring and rubbing soft fur against you when they are looking for a favor, and lashing out with claws and fangs when they don't get it. Your romantic idealism will only bring you grief.

A Gossip

Some gossiping can be fun. It turns ugly when it is used to hurt. Much of it comes terribly close to being slander or libel. Malicious gossip is a potent weapon because there is a ready market for bad news. The Bible assures us, "Without wood a fire goes out; without gossip a quarrel dies down" (Proverbs 26:20).

Nasty gossip is an expression of anger. There is no way we can compile statistics, but the odds favor as much injury being done to people with words as by guns and knives. Gossip hurts. Most of the damage gossip accomplishes is beyond repair. Paul lists it among the worst of sins. He is describing how the human choice to ignore God resulted in depravity.

> They are full of envy, murder, strife, deceit and malice. They are gossips, slanderers, God-haters, insolent, arrogant and boastful; they invent ways of doing evil.
> *Romans 1:29-30*

Gossips enjoy each other's company. They get together and trade stories that are either not worth keeping or too good to keep. The gossiping group actually feels superior to the ones who are being talked about. Sometimes they even have the audacity to say they are a prayer group. "Let's pray that God will quickly heal Martha's broken nose and that her husband won't hit her again."

There are no suggestions for how to make up with someone who has been slandering you with vicious gossip. You could possibly have them punished by law, but that is not the kind of reconciliation we are seeking in these pages. You can attempt to express your side of an issue, but the damage is likely to persist, and the gossipers are deriving too much pleasure and satisfaction from watching you squirm to repent. Leave them for Christ to judge.

A Crusader

These people are always right. If they hurt people, "they had it coming." Moral issues trigger their behavior. Instead of forgiving what they perceive as evil, they work to root it out.

Often groups of well-meaning people applaud their activity. Exposing and punishing sin becomes a satisfying and consuming hobby. "If God won't get them, I will!"

Jesus, in his parable, says that when the Prodigal Son returns home and his father is throwing the big celebration, his older brother asks what is going on.

> [He] became angry and refused to go in. So his father went out and pleaded with him. But he answered his father, "Look! All these years I've been slaving for you and never disobeyed your orders. Yet you never gave me even a young goat so I could celebrate with my friends. But when this son of yours who has squandered your property with prostitutes comes home, you kill the fattened calf for him!" *Luke 15:28-30*

A crusader believes he is on a noble quest. If you have been targeted, there is essentially nothing you can do to turn him into a friend. Nothing. Sorry. All you can do is wait for God to plow his garden with grief or personal suffering. Maybe, maybe then, there will be a slight opening for reconciliation to begin.

Impulsive

Some people make careful plans. Impulsive people speak or act first. Then they do their thinking. They are not known for using good judgment or having diplomatic skills. Neither are they burdened with hangups, taboos, and inhibitions. It is easy to make a point with them, if it is the right kind of point. They are quick to agree with you, and quick to disagree with you. They do not get lost in abstract thought. Offer them immediate gratification and they will grab it singing, "There's No Tomorrow!" They are suckers for the salesman who promises no payment until July.

Getting along with an impulsive person will keep you on your toes. They will never wonder if they are hurting anything or anyone. I can remember as a very young child being impressed by the balsa model airplane my brother was building. He had carefully glued together some 1/16" stringers on some 1/16" formers to make the fuselage and with balsa ribs and spars had built two small wings. When he got it all put together, I remember reaching out for it and taking it in my hand. It was the first time I had ever touched anything like it, and I squeezed it too tightly. The model airplane was crushed in my grip. It was an impulsive action. Many fights in bars start for no better reason. Sometimes it will be a comment at a committee meeting.

Since an impulsive person doesn't need a cause or a motive, you will have a difficult time trying to find something you can fix in your relationship. Believe it or not, it is possible for someone to be angry with you for no reason at all, at least not one they can identify. Ignoring or striking back are probably your only options. If you are being abused by an impulsive spouse, get help.

Antisocial

These people simply don't care about you and your feelings. Often criminals, they will hurt you with no remorse. They care only about themselves. If their pleasure brings you grief, what of it? The antisocial personalities who are not in jail are probably quite charming. They can be smooth enough to be called oily. Clever, inventive people, they feel no need to change even after they are in trouble. The ones who get into trouble with the law will have a long, long list of offenses. Lying comes as easily as breathing.

Apparently, antisocial individuals gave up trusting other people long ago. Pity the people who trust them. Let them work for you and they will steal everything they can. If you are married to one, you will never relax.

Prayer and love can help change an antisocial person. Religious conversion has resulted in some remarkable turnarounds. It is almost as though kindness and thoughtfulness are right there below the surface waiting to be let out. But until they are, an antisocial person is dangerous. Be careful. Keep a safe distance both emotionally and physically. Keep the door open to love and forgiveness, but let God perform the reconciliation you seek. Any other way you will get hurt.

Obstinate

An obstinate person is not open to anything new. He will carry his opinions to the grave. She continues a course of action even if it is clearly dangerous. Obstinacy does not yield to reason. No argument is persuasive enough. In the same way that certain illnesses do not respond to medications, the obstinate individual is stuck in a very deep rut. Dogged resistance to any alternate point of view and a stubborn refusal to accept any overture of compromise are typical indicators of a person beyond our best efforts at reconciliation.

That kind of description may lead you to think that an obstinate person is a blatantly hostile individual. Or perhaps you get a mental image of the child who takes his baseball and goes home when others refuse to play the game his way. Sometimes these are applicable. But quite often obstinacy resides in a person whose face never reddens with anger.

Jesus dealt with such a person. Our Lord, an extraordinarily attractive man, drew all kinds of people to himself wherever he went. We have no idea what he looked like. There is not one word of physical description by his contemporaries in existence anywhere. We can be sure he was nothing like the actors who play him by drifting around silently and staring at people until they get converted. It is his ideas that turn people on. His divine insight into the largest questions ever asked by religion are fresh and invigorating. "The crowds were amazed at his teaching, because he taught as one who had authority, and not as their teachers of the law" (Matthew 7:28-29).

People who were exposed to Jesus began to ask themselves what kind of dreams God had for them. He was introducing something strange and dynamic into the spiritual lives of everyone. Impossibilities were becoming almost easy. Things that had seemed as distant as the stars came into reach of ordinary people. It is not surprising that he attracted crowds. It is no wonder many looked for a way to spend a few minutes in private conversation with him.

One day a man ran up to Jesus. He fell down on his knees in front of him. Since it is known that he was a man of wealth and authority, the running and the kneeling are surprising. Important people don't run in public unless they are jogging or joining the pack in a ten-miler or marathon. Soldiers of rank used to be sternly cautioned against running on the battlefield. If you are in charge, you walk no matter what kind of shells, bombs and bullets are incoming. Walk fast, if you must, but never, ever run. Something urgent was going on inside the man who ran up to Jesus. He saw an opportunity and he seized it with enthusiasm.

Kneeling before Jesus may have been an impulsive act. As a VIP, the rich man would often have had other people kneeling at his feet. In the East, common people knelt before their rulers when they had a request or wanted to express gratitude. Here we see the spectacle of a wealthy ruler kneeling before a peasant, a shocking thing in that time and place.

There is something in this man's attitude toward Jesus that shows a lot of courage. His peers were not supportive of Jesus' ministry. Many other influential people were openly hostile. A public display of this kind exposed him to great personal risk.

" 'Good teacher,' he asked, 'what must I do to inherit eternal life?' " (Mark 10:17)

As much as he had, he was conscious of something lacking in himself. If it were for sale, he would already have it. If it could be his by pulling the right strings, he had all the connections. If decency had anything to do with it, it would be within his grasp. But the emptiness in him was inescapable. His life lacked purpose and meaning. There was a quality in Jesus that fascinated him. He wanted it for himself. He may have found it difficult to articulate precisely the nature of his longing, but he knew God had something to do with it, and he recognized God in Christ. "What must I do?"

"You know the commandments: 'Do not murder, do not commit adultery, do not steal, do not give false testimony, do not defraud, honor your father and mother' " (Mark 10:19).

Jesus selects the last six of the Ten Commandments, the ones that apply to human relationships. (The first four cover our relationship with God.) The effect is something like that of walking into six dark, private rooms and turning on the lights. Most of us would quite naturally be a little rattled by this. But this man is not.

" 'Teacher,' he declared, 'all these things I have kept since I was a boy' " (Mark 10:20). In all probability he was telling the truth. He was not only rich and prominent; he was clean.

The Gospels tell us that Jesus looked at him and loved him. It was an expression of respect. He accepted the accuracy of the man's comment. He perceived the pain of his longing spirit. He saw that this seeker was primed and ready. Spiritual hunger was clearly evident. He also knew this one wasn't going to be easy.

" 'One thing you lack,' he said. 'Go, sell everything you have and give to the poor, and you will have treasure in heaven. Then come, follow me' " (Mark 10:21).

Are we to understand that the thing the man lacked was poverty? I don't think so. His lack was the perception of God in Christ reconciling the world to himself. At the center of his life he was still missing God as the dominant influence. Love of God and God's children did not yet burn in his heart. "You need God. Follow me."

"At this the man's face fell. He went away sad, because he had great wealth" (Mark 10:22). He had run to Jesus with great enthusiasm. Now he departs crestfallen.

We don't know the rest of this story. It could be that this man went home, thought it over, bit the bullet, and did exactly what Jesus had recommended. The narrative leaves us with the impression that this didn't happen. If we are keeping score, this one does not go in the win column. Obstinacy, whether it is strong-willed and determined or mildly hesitant, is an almost insurmountable obstacle to reconciliation. Even so, we should not give up too soon, for as Christ said to his disciples after this saddened man went away, "All things are possible with God" (Mark 10:27).

The Burden Is on You

People with character disorders find it difficult to accept or return genuine love. When you become involved with them, your own expressions of love can have a negative effect that will surprise and frustrate you. This could be what Jesus was warning us about when he said, "Do not give dogs what is sacred; do not throw your pearls to pigs. If you do, they may trample them under their feet, and then turn and tear you to pieces" (Matthew 7:6).

Reconciliation is sometimes a one-sided thing. You may simply have to learn to respect certain other people for who they are and be satisfied with that. Remind yourself that someone is hiding behind that barrier of a character disorder. A sugary, sentimental, idealistic kind of love will not reach that secret person. The only expression of love that is useful is what has come to be called "tough love." This is a secular expression of what Christianity has always called *agapē* love. It is the kind of caring for another person that can't be discouraged by rejection because it is not looking for anything in return. The more of this kind of love you give, the larger your supply of it becomes. It does not play up to difficult people, tiptoeing through an emotional mine field. That only spoils them. *Agapē* love has the power of Christ that can transform them into whole, integrated personalities.

Agapē love does not panic or get into a sweat. It is patient and kind.

It does not envy, it does not boast, it is not proud. It is not rude, it is not self-seeking, it is not easily angered, it keeps no record of wrongs. . . . It always protects, always trusts, always hopes, always perseveres.
1 Corinthians 13:4-7

Human character develops amid crisis and challenge. Our task is to give other people the stimulation to grow, but whether they make progress or revert to immaturity is out of our hands.

Bless those who persecute you; bless and do not curse.
Romans 12:14

12

THE WAY CHRIST RECOVERED A FRIEND

> When he saw the crowds, he had compassion on them, because they were harassed and helpless, like sheep without a shepherd. Then he said to his disciples, "The harvest is plentiful but the workers are few. Ask the Lord of the harvest, therefore, to send out workers into his harvest field."
>
> *Matthew 9:36-38*

e have examined various aspects of getting along with others. Most of us have many opportunities in a lifetime to patch up broken relationships. Sometimes we are successful; sometimes we fail. Ultimately it comes down not to technique, but to caring. The best path to reconciliation is love. There is no better way to learn how this operates in human relationships than by observing love at work.

The acknowledged master in understanding and dealing with people is Jesus Christ. He has a way of resolving conflict, answering questions, and pointing out better alternatives that is simply amazing. Once he got caught up in a life-and-death situation with a crowd of emotional and violent men. They had caught a woman in the act of adultery. The law of Moses allowed her to be executed in public by stoning. When they asked him his opinion, he replied, "If any one of you is without sin, let him be the first to throw a stone at her" (John 8:7). One by one, the men went away. In many other instances we can see Jesus getting to the heart of the matter, pushing aside all the emotionally encumbered side issues, and helping people determine what is important in a relationship.

Jesus always puts his teaching into action; he practices what he preaches. He demonstrates with his own life the way human relationships are enriched and reconciled when God is a part of the process. In this closing chapter, let's take a look first at one of Christ's most popular parables, and then see how he applied it in his own experience. The little sermon-story is the one we call "The Parable of the Prodigal Son."

What Jesus Taught

It begins with a separation. It opens with an explosion of independence that disintegrates the close ties between father and son. "Father, give me my share of the estate" (Luke 15:12). Home is stifling the son. He dreams of a bigger world out there, a place where he can be on his own. He is tired of having people worry about him when he gets in late at night. He doesn't want to answer stressful questions about his friends. He has a perfectly normal desire to be responsible for his own life, and it has probably broken through to the surface right on schedule.

Of course, he is naive. As a young man he is fairly ignorant of the ways of the world. Inexperienced. There are all kinds of traps and hazards waiting for him out there. In our families today the conversation would probably go something like this:

"Dad, I'm ready to move on. This town doesn't offer me any opportunities. I want to go someplace that's on the map. I've heard they're making big money in California. If you would give me enough money to get me started, I'll soon be on my own."

"Son, you don't know what you're getting into. California can be a difficult and expensive place for a young man to live."

"I can take care of myself. I don't need all the things you and Mom have. I think I can really be myself out there."

"But there are so many details! Life is more complicated than putting gas in your car. Where will you stay? Who do you know in California? You can't live long on hamburgers and fries. What about insurance?"

"Hey, Dad, I'm a big boy now. I can take care of things. Just give me some money to get started."

"No, Son. I beg you. Please think this thing through. You don't know what you're getting into. Don't go. It's too risky. Jim Brinkley got mugged in L.A. Wally Gresham got AIDS. I can't let you go."

But that is not the way Jesus tells it. The son asks for his share of the inheritance, and without comment the father gives it to him. The son wants to break away from home, and the father lets him go. No big scene.

Resistance is not likely to produce anything but resentment anyway. Love is not something that can be forced. It must be freely given, or it isn't love. Healthy home and family relationships are natural things, existing on a plane far above what can be controlled and coerced. I remember encountering a fretful child on the rim of Yellowstone Canyon. The falls and the river gorge were awesomely impressive, but the little girl was not able to take it all in. She had some other need that was not being met. Her exasperated mother took her by the shoulders, shook her, and said, "I brought you here to have a good time. Now you have a good time!" She really said that, and I think she meant it. Arguing and pleading with the son who thinks he is ready to leave home changes nothing. Insisting that he stay against his will does nothing to make him feel any more at home. In Jesus' parable, the father gave the younger son what he was seeking. He was free to go. No strings.

But a valuable bond is broken. In an act of self-will that shows little regard for the feelings or wisdom of others, the young man has severed his ties with home. He "got together all he had, set off for a distant country and there squandered his wealth in wild living" (Luke 15:13). We can be sure there was no communication with home during this time. Today, there would be no phone calls, no letters. His family was left to guess about where he was and how he was doing. Most parents have no difficulty imagining such things. The emotional burden must have been devastating. No doubt there was a kind of mourning going on. Grieving. After a while, the folks at home would not have known whether he was dead or alive. They could only hope and pray.

What had started as a fun-filled blast quickly turned sour. The boy had gone out looking for pleasure, but soon enough he found pain. "After he had spent everything, there was a severe famine in that whole country, and he began to be in need" (Luke 15:14). The advance inheritance is gone. It hasn't bought anything of permanent investment value. He has nothing to show for his spending spree except an empty moneybag and a headache. The "friends" who have helped him spend it are gone. Simple survival now becomes a problem for this homeless young man.

"So he went and hired himself out to a citizen of that country, who sent him to his fields to feed pigs" (Luke 15:15). Only a Jew or an Arab can feel the disgusting nature of this job. This is worse than cleaning latrines. There is no more demeaning employment than this on earth for the young man in the parable. "He longed to fill his stomach with the pods that the pigs were eating, but no one gave him anything" (Luke 15:16).

I have tried to help a lot of young people in similar situations. Some have a problem with alcohol and drugs. Others are addicted to clandestine relationships. A few can't seem to control their temper and are wearing home relationships thin. Still others have difficulty managing finances. In almost every case, there is little to be done until the individual comes face-to-face with the consequences of irresponsible behavior. They literally have to "hit bottom." All of the tearful prayers of those who love them and are committed to them will not make any difference until the subject of those prayers reaches a point of utter helplessness. Until then, they will not admit they have a problem. "I can control it," they will say. When the Prodigal hit bottom, "he came to his senses [and] said, 'How many of my father's hired men have food to spare, and here I am starving to death!' " (Luke 15:17).

So he makes up a little speech.

"I will set out and go back to my father and say to him: Father, I have sinned against heaven and against you. I am no longer worthy to be called your son; make me like one of your hired men." *Luke 15:18-19*

It is a humble, contrite, apologetic, and manipulative statement. First, get Dad's sympathy. Disarm his wrath. Then make a deal. "Don't take me back as a son. I've given up my right to that. Let me go to work for you. I'll earn my keep."

In one of the truly pretty touches of Christ's story-telling technique, the young man never has an opportunity to negotiate the terms of his acceptance. Instead of discovering a bitter father who is reluctant to reestablish their broken relationship, he is confronted with the very opposite. "While he was still a long way off, his father saw him and was filled with compassion for him; he ran to his son, threw his arms around him and kissed him" (Luke 15:20). The son immediately begins the little speech he had prepared. It does not exactly seem right in this hugging context, but he has programmed himself to say it. The memorized words roll out, "Father, I have sinned against heaven and against you. I am no longer worthy to be called your son" (Luke 14:21).

But the father doesn't let him finish his spiel. He cuts him off with directions to his servants to go and get some decent clothes and shoes for his son. And food! Lots of food! The boy is skin and bones! Instead of hearing the part about "make me like one of your hired men," the father's enthusiasm and joy overwhelm the moment. "Let's have a feast and celebrate. For this son of mine was dead and is alive again; he was lost and is found" (Luke 15:23-24).

This, then, is Christ's most picturesque teaching about the restoration of a broken relationship. He tells us in an unforgettable story, a story of the way genuine love makes reconciliation happen. Now let's see him apply his idea in a broken relationship of his own.

What Jesus Did

Like any charismatic personality, Jesus had ardent supporters and venomous detractors. It is almost a laughable under-statement to say that at the end, when he was crucified, he did not have much support from his closest friends. Most of his disciples vanished. Only John, his mother, Mary Magdalene, and a couple of other women were at Calvary to witness the crucifixion.

In particular, Simon Peter was a great disappointment. When Jesus was arrested, Peter's faith evaporated. After three years of grooming, he proved to be a worthless supporter. Trembling with spineless fear, he denied his Lord and protected his own interests. It is one of the greatest letdowns in history.

Jesus had much hope for him, saw vast potential in him, said encouraging and hopeful things about him, and took him as one of his closest friends and confidants. But when the chips were down Peter swore he had never even met his Lord.

Still, Jesus was not content to let him fall away. His confidence in Peter remained. It is clear from reading the Gospel accounts of the activity of Jesus following the first Easter Sunday that recovering this failure of a disciple was one of his primary objectives.

The first hint of this priority can be seen in what happened at the empty tomb on Easter morning. The two angels at the tomb told the women, "He has risen! He is not here. See the place where they laid him. But go, tell his disciples and

Peter" (Mark 16:6-7). There is a specific message in that for the lost disciple: "his disciples *and Peter.*" It is a message of forgiveness, of grace. It is an open invitation to reconciliation. The women could have figured that anyone who had denied he had ever seen or known Jesus could no longer be counted among the disciples. To prevent any mistake about this, the women are directed to make it clear to Simon Peter that he was to be included. Christ does not forget his friends even when they forget him. He sends a special message to call us back.

From Luke's account of Easter, we can infer that Christ appeared to Peter in private. When the two who had walked with him on the road to Emmaus returned to Jerusalem, where the disciples were gathered together, they say, "It is true! The Lord has risen and has appeared to Simon" (Luke 24:34). In his list of resurrection appearances, Paul also puts Peter first. "He appeared to Peter, and then to the Twelve" (1 Corinthians 15:5). Of all the appearances, this is the one we would like to know the most about. But it never got written down. Perhaps it was too private, too sacred to share.

The next step to recovering Peter as a friend and fellow worker was our Lord's conversation with him that remarkable morning on the shore of the Sea of Galilee. The Bible's last mention of Simon Peter prior to this was at night with the predawn crowing of a rooster piercing his heart. Having denied his Lord, he went out and wept bitterly. Now it is morning, another day, another place. We can read about this moment on the last page of the Gospel of John. Seven of the disciples have returned to the Sea of Galilee to resume their old trade as fishermen.

All through the night Peter, Thomas, Nathanael, the sons of Zebedee, James and John, and two others who are unnamed have been fishing with no luck. In the first light of dawn, they head for shore with empty nets. They see an individual on the beach who calls out to them. "Friends, haven't you any fish?"

"No," they answered.

When the stranger directs them to cast their net on the right side of the boat, Peter instantly recognizes who it is. "It is the Lord!" At that, impulsive Peter did exactly what we would expect him to do. He jumped into the water and swam and waded the remaining hundred yards or so to shore. The others soon joined him, and they began a simple meal of fish and bread. Nobody could think of much to say. John expresses it this way. "None of the disciples dared ask him, 'Who are you?' They knew it was the Lord" (John 21:12).

Probably there were six men present who were wondering what Jesus would say to Peter. Perhaps it would go like this: "How could you have done it? You denied me! Do you still think you are fit to be one of my disciples? What is the difference between your sin and the sin of Judas?"

But they hear nothing like that. When Jesus speaks to Peter after breakfast there is not one single reference to the past. Instead, Jesus asks Peter this: "Do you love me?" Three times he had denied his Lord. Now three times he is given an opportunity to affirm his love. The past is blotted out. His sin is forgiven and forgotten. Peter is restored to his place as an apostle. He is given another chance.

In the process, Jesus discourages a wounded spirit from despising itself. He does not allow room for a pity party, or for groveling in self-hatred. Jesus demonstrates great skill in helping Peter to focus his attention on what really matters. And what matters is where we go from here—not where we have been. Peter had hurt someone he loved. There is no sharper pain or deeper remorse than that. With the delicate touch of a surgeon, Jesus removes the obstacle that stands between him and this important team member. "Do you love me? I've got work for you to do. Do you love me?"

In the language of television producers, Peter is given a new time slot. He gets to start another program without any reference to the one that got canned. Not only is his sin forgiven, but he is granted a great commission and sent forth on a mission to preach the gospel and feed Christ's sheep.

If Christ were to speak this way to any of the other six who are with him that morning for breakfast on the beach, it would not seem strange. Even if he were to single out skeptical Thomas, who had openly expressed his doubts about the Resurrection and insisted on firsthand evidence, it would not be surprising. The astonishing thing is that he says it to Peter. And look at the results! Suddenly the man with such a weak and undependable character becomes a primary leader in the early Christian church. He is no longer bumbling and impulsive. He has new courage and boldness in the Lord. He becomes a dedicated evangelist and organizer, tossing to the winds any concern for his own personal safety. Christ and Peter are reconciled.

Only a few of us are gifted in the art of diplomacy. Most of us have to work hard to keep our relationships at home, at work, at play, and in voluntary organizations running smoothly. We say things we do not mean and take actions we regret. Sometimes we make a mess of things simply by using the wrong word and triggering an emotional response. If we were to admit the truth, we are probably more like Simon Peter than Jesus Christ.

But genuine reconciliation takes two participants. In love, the one must forgive sincerely and naturally. In love, the other needs to be open to acceptance and able to cope with generosity. When we are able to put these Christian principles into practice, life becomes more pleasant for everyone. Apply them regularly for enough time and they will become a natural part of your way of living with others. You simply will not feel a snub or nurse a grudge. With Christ at your side you may get hurt, but you will not need to get even.

APPENDIX

Questions to Ask Yourself in Conflict

The guidance offered in this book is intended for consideration by people who are engaged in nonviolent conflict. Sometimes we are not aware when the fight has escalated beyond a simple contest and become something that is significantly damaging to all participants. This is particularly true of domestic struggles, where bonds of blood and love disguise the truth and distort our vision of reality. Violence at home does not always draw blood. Here are some important questions to ask yourself. Does someone you love:

- "Track" all of your time?

- Constantly accuse you of being unfaithful?

- Discourage your relationships with family and friends?

- Prevent you from working or attending school?

- Criticize you for little things?

- Anger easily when drinking or on drugs?

- Control all finances and force you to account for what you spend?

- Humiliate you in front of others?

- Destroy personal property and sentimental items?

- Hit, punch, slap, kick, or bite you or your children?

- Threaten to hurt you or your children?

- Use or threaten to use a weapon against you?

- Force you to have sex against your will?

If you can answer more than one or two questions like these affirmatively, it may be advisable for you to seek outside help. The National Coalition Against Domestic Violence will help you find a program in your area. Call 1-303-839-1852.

Mediation Centers

Many communities today have mediation centers. These are nonprofit organizations staffed largely by trained volunteers.

They have perfected a method of listening to all sides of an argument that can bring positive, speedy results. The process and the goals are quite different from arbitration and adjudication, in which disputants ask a third party to make decisions for them. Mediation places the responsibility for determining the outcome upon the disputants themselves. Each participant retains full control. All sides agree not to interrupt each other as a trained mediator listens. The participants are then helped to find a mutually satisfying agreement. Almost any kind of dispute is accepted. There is usually a small fee for the service. Look for such an organization in your neighborhood in the phone book under names such as "Community Mediation Center," "Dispute Resolution Center," "Conflict Resolution Service," or "Dispute Settlement Center."

Other Helpful Organizations

Other organizations that may be helpful to you as resources after reading this book are listed below.

Lebow Company. A national training and consulting firm that specializes in promoting shared values, empowerment and team-building. 1-800-423-9327 or 1-206-828-3509.

The Alban Institute, Inc. Founded in 1974 to research congregational life, The Alban Institute is a unique ecumenical resource for congregations that provides practical help through publications, on-site counsulting or training services, and continuing education programs. 1-800-242-5226 or 1-202-244-7320.

Parents Anonymous Hotline. A free service for parents who are overwhelmed and are looking for better ways to resolve conflict. 1-800-421-0353 or 212-388-6685 or 1-800-775-1134.

National Child Abuse Hotline. Children may call. 1-800-422-4453.

National Association for Christian Recovery. For religious help with the pain of unresolved conflict and trauma. 1-310-697-6201.